SPECTRUM
Test Practice

Grade 2

Spectrum

An imprint of Carson-Dellosa Publishing LLC
Greensboro, North Carolina

Spectrum
An imprint of Carson-Dellosa Publishing LLC
P.O. Box 35665
Greensboro, NC 27425 USA

Printed in the USA • All rights reserved.   ISBN: 1-57768-722-1

9 10 11 12 13 14 PAH 15 14 13 12 11 10

SPECTRUM TEST PRACTICE
Table of Contents
Grade 2

With increased accountability in ensuring academic success for all learners, testing now takes a significant amount of time for students in all settings. Standardized tests are designed to measure what students know. These tests are nationally normed. State tests are usually tied to specific academic standards identified for mastery.

For many students, testing can be a mystery. They fear not doing well and not knowing what to expect on the test. This *Spectrum Test Practice* book was developed to introduce students to both the format and the content they will encounter on tests. It was developed on the assumption that students have received prior instruction on the skills included. This book is designed to cover the content on a representative sample of state standards. The sampling of standards is found on pages 8–10 with a correlation to the skills covered in this book and a correlation to sample standardized tests. Spaces are provided to record the correlation to the tests being administered by the user of this book. Spaces are also provided to add standards that are specific to the user.

Features of *Spectrum Test Practice*

- Skill lessons, sample tests for subtopics, and comprehensive content area tests
- Clues for being successful with specific skills
- Correlation of skills to state standards and standardized tests
- Format and structure similar to other formal tests
- Written response required in the Science and Social Studies sections
- Reproducible for use by a teacher for a classroom

Overview

This book is developed within content areas (Reading, Language, Math, Science, and Social Studies). A comprehensive practice test follows at the end of the content area, with an answer sheet for students to record responses. Within each content area, specific subtopics have been identified. Sample tests are provided for each subtopic. Within each subtopic, specific skill lessons are presented. These specific skill lessons include an example and a clue for being successful with the skill.

Comprehensive Practice Test

A comprehensive practice test is provided for each content area. The subtopics for each area are identified below:

- **Reading**
  - Word Analysis (letter sounds, rhyming words, word study, contractions and compound words, and root words and suffixes)
  - Vocabulary (picture vocabulary, word meaning, synonyms, antonyms, multiple meaning words, and words in context)
  - Reading Comprehension (picture comprehension, critical reading, fiction and nonfiction articles)

- **Language**
  - Listening Skills
  - Language Mechanics (capitalization and punctuation)
  - Language Expression (pronouns, adjectives, sentences, and paragraphs)
  - Spelling (both correct and incorrect spelling)
  - Study Skills (dictionary skills, book parts, and map reading)

- **Math**
  - Concepts (numeration, number concepts, patterns, and properties)
  - Computation (addition and subtraction of whole numbers, introduction of multiplication and division facts)
  - Applications (geometry, measurement, and problem solving)
- **Science***
  - Water Cycle
  - Weather
  - Plant and Animal Structures
- **Social Studies***
  - Geography Terms/Concepts
  - Introduction to the Constitution
  - Economics

*Since states and often districts determine units of study within Science and Social Studies, the content in this book may not be aligned with the content offered in all courses of study. The content within each area is grade level appropriate. It is based on a sampling of state standards. The tests in Science and Social Studies include both multiple choice and written answer.

Comprehensive Practice Test Includes

- Content Area (i.e. Language)
- Subtopics (i.e. Language Mechanics)
- Directions, examples, and test questions
- Separate answer sheet with "bubbles" to be filled in for answers

Sample Tests

Sample tests are included for all subtopics. These sample tests are designed to apply the knowledge and experience from the skill lessons in a more formal format. These sample tests are

shorter than the comprehensive tests and longer than the skill lessons. The skills on the test items are presented in the same order as introduced in the book.

Sample Tests Include

- Subtopic (i.e. Language Mechanics)
- Directions, examples, and test questions

Skill Lessons

Skill lessons include sample questions and clues for mastering the skill. The questions are formatted as they generally appear in tests, whether the tests are standardized and nationally normed or state specific.

Skill Lessons Include

- Subtopic (i.e. Language Mechanics)
- Skill (i.e. Punctuation)
- Directions and examples
- Clues for completing the activity
- Practice questions

Use

This book can be used in a variety of ways, depending on the needs of the students. Some examples follow:

- Review the skills correlation on pages 8–10. Record the skills tested in your state and/or district on the blanks provided.
- Administer the comprehensive practice test for each content area. Have students use the sample answer sheet in order to simulate the actual testing experience. The tests for Reading, Language, and Math are multiple choice. Evaluate the results.
- Administer the sample test for the subtopics within the content area. Evaluate the results.

- Administer the specific skill lessons for those students needing additional practice with content. Evaluate the results.

- Use the skill lessons as independent work in centers, for homework, or as seatwork.

- Prepare an overhead transparency of skill lessons to be presented to a group of students. Use the transparency to model the skill and provide guided practice.

- Send home the Letter to Parent/Guardian found on page 7.

Clues for Getting Started

- Determine the structure for implementing *Spectrum Test Practice*. These questions may help guide you:

  - Do you want to assess the overall performance of your class in each academic area? If so, reproduce the practice test and sample answer sheet for each area. Use the results to determine subtopics that need additional instruction and/or practice.

  - Do you already have information about the overall achievement of your students within each academic area? Do you need more information about their achievement within subtopics, such as Vocabulary within Reading? If so, reproduce the sample tests for the subtopics.

  - Do your students need additional practice with some of the specific skills that they will encounter on the standardized test? Do you need to know which students have mastered which skills? These skill lessons provide opportunities for instruction and practice.

- Go over the purpose of tests with your students. Describe the tests and the testing situation, explaining that the tests are often timed, that answers are recorded on a separate answer sheet, and that the questions cover material they have studied.

- Do some of the skill lessons together to help students develop strategies for selecting answers and for different types of questions. Use the "clues" for learning strategies for test taking.

- Make certain that students know how to mark a separate answer sheet. Use the practice test and answer sheet so that they are familiar with the process.

- Review the directions for each test. Identify key words that students must use to answer the questions. Do the sample test questions with the class.

- Remind students to answer each question, to budget their time so they can complete all the questions, and to apply strategies for determining answers.

Reduce the mystery of taking tests for your students. By using *Spectrum Test Practice*, you have the materials that show them what the tests will look like, what kinds of questions are on the tests, and ways to help them be more successful taking tests.

Note: Determine the structure that best fits your class. Many portions of these tests may need to be read to your students. Use the same procedure that is used on state or standardized tests to provide the best practice for your students.

Note: If you wish to time your students on a practice test, we suggest allowing 1.25 minutes per question for this grade level.

Dear Parent/Guardian:

We will be giving tests to measure your child's learning. These tests include questions that relate to the information your child is learning in school. The tests may be standardized and used throughout the nation, or they may be specific to our state. Regardless of the test, the results are used to measure student achievement.

Many students do not test well even though they know the material. They may not test well because of test anxiety or the mystery of taking tests. What will the test look like? What will some of the questions be? What happens if I do not do well?

To help your child do his/her best on the tests, we will be using some practice tests These tests help your child learn what the tests will look like, what some of the questions might be, and ways to learn to take tests. These practice tests will be included as part of your child's homework.

You can help your child with this important part of learning. Below are some suggestions:

- Ask your child if he/she has homework.
- Provide a quiet place to work.
- Go over the work with your child.
- Use a timer to help your child learn to manage his/her time when taking tests.
- Tell your child he/she is doing a good job.
- Remind him/her to use the clues that are included in the lessons.

If your child is having difficulty with the tests, these ideas may be helpful:

- Review the examples.
- Skip the difficult questions and come back to them later.
- Guess at those that you do not know.
- Answer all the questions.

By showing you are interested in how your child is doing, he/she will do even better in school. Enjoy this time with your child. Good luck with the practice tests.

Sincerely,

● **Grade 2**

Sample Standards	Spectrum Test Practice Gr. 2	*CAT Level for Gr. 2	**CTBS Level for Gr. 2	Other	Other	Other
Reading						
Word Analysis						
Recognizing Beginning, Medial, and Ending Sounds	x	x	x			
Recognizing Rhyming Words	x					
Recognizing Compound Words	x	x	x			
Recognizing Contractions	x	x	x			
Recognizing Root Words and Suffixes	x	x	x			
Other						
Other						
Vocabulary						
Using Synonyms	x	x	x			
Using Antonyms	x		x			
Matching Pictures to Words	x	x	x			
Using Multiple Meaning Words	x					
Using Context Clues	x	x	x			
Other						
Other						
Comprehension						
Identifying Main Idea	x	x	x			
Identifying Supporting Details	x	x	x			
Identifying Sequence of Events	x	x				
Drawing Conclusions	x	x	x			
Making Predictions	x	x	x			
Comparing and Contrasting	x					
Identifying Cause and Effect	x		x			
Identifying Character Traits/Feelings	x	x	x			
Distinguishing Between Fact and Opinion	x					
Distinguishing Between Reality and Fantasy	x					
Using Graphic Organizers						
Summarizing	x	x				
Identifying Author's Purpose	x					
Reading Various Genres			x			
Other						
Other						
Language						
Mechanics						
Expression						
Using Correct Capitalization and Punctuation	x	x	x			
Determining Correct Usage	x	x	x			
Recognizing Complete Sentences	x		x			
Other						
Other						

* Terra Nova CAT™   ©2001 CTB/McGraw-Hill
** Terra Nova CTBS®   ©1997 CTB/McGraw-Hill

Grade 2

Sample Standards

Sample Standards	Spectrum Test Practice Gr. 2	*CAT Level for Gr. 2	**CTBS Level for Gr. 2	Other	Other	Other
Spelling						
Identifying Correct Spelling	x					
Identifying Incorrect Spelling	x					
Other						
Study Skills						
Using Reference Materials	x					
Using Book Parts	x					
Using Graphic Organizers						
Other						
Math						
Concepts						
Numeration	x					
Using Number Lines	x		x			
Using Numbers Up to 100	x	x	x			
Ordering and Comparing Whole Numbers	x		x			
Using Place Value	x	x	x			
Other						
Algebra						
Recognizing Patterns with Pictures	x	x	x			
Extending Number Patterns	x	x	x			
Using Number Sentences	x	x	x			
Using Symbols To Represent Numbers		x				
Other						
Other						
Fractions and Decimals						
Recognizing Fractions and Decimals from Pictures (fractions only)	x	x				
Other						
Computation						
Whole Numbers						
Solving Two-Digit Addition and Subtraction Problems With and Without Regrouping	x	x	x			
Using Mental Math for Adding and Subtracting Rounded Numbers						
Estimating	x		x			
Other						
Probability						
Collecting Data			x			
Other						

* Terra Nova CAT™ ©2001 CTB/McGraw-Hill
** Terra Nova CTBS® ©1997 CTB/McGraw-Hill

● **Grade 2**

Sample Standards

	Spectrum Test Practice Gr. 2	*CAT Level for Gr. 2	**CTBS Level for Gr. 2	Other	Other	Other
Applications						
Geometry						
Identifying Shapes	X	X	X			
Identifying Lines of Symmetry	X		X			
Identifying Congruent Figures	X					
Other						
Other						
Measurement						
Estimating	X	X				
Measuring to the Nearest Inch and Centimeter	X	X				
Recognizing Relationships of Feet and Inches/Meters and Centimeters						
Finding Perimeter and Area of Squares and Rectangles (perimeter only)	X					
Using Volume, Mass, and Capacity			X			
Telling Time to the Quarter Hour	X		X			
Finding Value of Coins	X	X	X			
Other						
Problem Solving						
Selecting Appropriate Operations	X	X	X			
Using a Variety of Methods to Solve Problems, Including Graphs, Tables, and Charts	X	X	X			
Estimating Results			X			
Selecting Reasonable Solutions						
Other						
Science						
Using the Scientific Method			X			
Understanding Plant and Animal Features	X	X	X			
Understanding Properties of Materials	X	X	X			
Understanding the Water Cycle	X		X			
Understanding the Types of Matter	X	X				
Other						
Social Studies						
Comparing Life in the Past and Present		X	X			
Identifying Rights and Responsibilities	X		X			
Locating Community and U.S. on Maps			X			
Identifying Land Forms	X	X				
Applying the Basic Vocabulary of Economics		X				
Developing Time Lines						
Other						

* Terra Nova CAT™   ©2001 CTB/McGraw-Hill
** Terra Nova CTBS®   ©1997 CTB/McGraw-Hill

Name _____   Date _____

READING: WORD ANALYSIS

● **Lesson 1: Word Sounds**

Directions: Choose the best answer to each question.

Example

A. **Which word has the same beginning sound as sheep?**

   Ⓐ chin

   Ⓑ shake

   Ⓒ seven

   Ⓓ sleep

 Clue Read all the answer choices before choosing the one you think is correct.

● **Practice**

1. **Which word has the same beginning sound as blue?**

   Ⓐ blast

   Ⓑ boy

   Ⓒ brush

   Ⓓ few

2. **Which word has the same vowel sound as join?**

   Ⓕ tool

   Ⓖ joke

   Ⓗ spoil

   Ⓙ cold

3. **Which word has the same ending sound as from?**

   Ⓐ float

   Ⓑ barn

   Ⓒ come

   Ⓓ fry

4. **Which word has the same vowel sound as found?**

   Ⓕ down

   Ⓖ flood

   Ⓗ road

   Ⓙ could

5. **Which word has the same ending sound as spend?**

   Ⓐ seen

   Ⓑ pound

   Ⓒ pain

   Ⓓ spot

6. **Which word has the same beginning sound as another?**

   Ⓕ about

   Ⓖ arm

   Ⓗ clue

   Ⓙ ace

 STOP

READING: WORD ANALYSIS

● **Lesson 2: Rhyming Words**

Directions: Choose the best answer to each question.

Example

A. Which picture rhymes with the word **fun**?

(A)

(B)

(C)

Clue If you are not sure which answer is correct, take your best guess.

● **Practice**

1. Which picture rhymes with the word **seal**?

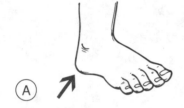
(A)

(B)

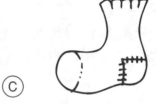
(C)

2. Which picture rhymes with the word **bag**?

(F)

(G)

(H)

3. Which picture rhymes with the word **five**?

(A)

(B)

(C)

4. Which picture rhymes with the word **honey**?

(F)

(G)

(H)

STOP

READING: WORD ANALYSIS

● **Lesson 3: Word Sounds**

Directions: Choose the word that has the same sound as the underlined part of the word.

Examples

A. This one has been done for you.
<u>u</u>mbrella

- (A) use
- (B) cube
- (●) skunk
- (D) four

B. Practice this one with your teacher.
gro<u>wl</u>

- (F) food
- (G) couch
- (H) home
- (J) grow

Clue Match the sound of the underlined letter or letters. Look at each answer choice and say each answer choice quietly to yourself.

● **Practice**

1. **c<u>a</u>me**
   - (A) rain
   - (B) hand
   - (C) black
   - (D) swam

2. **h<u>er</u>**
   - (F) fire
   - (G) real
   - (H) here
   - (J) turn

3. **<u>ea</u>sy**
   - (A) child
   - (B) keep
   - (C) ten
   - (D) head

4. **<u>g</u>ood**
   - (F) sound
   - (G) but
   - (H) could
   - (J) hold

5. **thi<u>s</u>**
   - (A) their
   - (B) still
   - (C) kind
   - (D) mine

6. **<u>c</u>oat**
   - (F) know
   - (G) out
   - (H) people
   - (J) school

STOP

READING: WORD ANALYSIS

● Lesson 4: Rhyming Words

Directions: Choose the answer that rhymes with each word.

Examples

A. mop

- Ⓐ book
- Ⓑ cap
- Ⓒ top

B. car

- Ⓐ cat
- Ⓑ star
- Ⓒ bear

 Clue Say the words to yourself. Listen to the sounds.

● Practice

1. dog

- Ⓐ duck
- Ⓑ pig
- Ⓒ frog
- Ⓓ bag

2. hat

- Ⓕ hand
- Ⓖ heart
- Ⓗ cat
- Ⓙ tap

3. rock

- Ⓐ sock
- Ⓑ home
- Ⓒ spoon
- Ⓓ bake

4. ride

- Ⓕ street
- Ⓖ slide
- Ⓗ chip
- Ⓙ pie

STOP

READING: WORD ANALYSIS

● **Lesson 5: Contractions and Compound Words**

Directions: Choose the best answer to each question.

Examples

A. Which word is a compound word, a word that is made up of two smaller words?

- (A) footprint
- (B) remember
- (C) narrow
- (D) explain

B. Look at the word. Find the answer that tells what the contraction means.
aren't

- (F) are not
- (G) are late
- (H) are most
- (J) are then

 Clue If a question is too difficult, skip it and come back to it later.

● **Practice**

1. Which word is a compound word?
   - (A) repeat
   - (B) follow
   - (C) shopping
   - (D) outside

2. Which word is a compound word?
   - (F) introduce
   - (G) overpass
   - (H) describe
   - (J) unnecessary

3. Which word is a compound word?
   - (A) being
   - (B) enough
   - (C) family
   - (D) everyone

4. **don't**
   - (F) did it
   - (G) drive in
   - (H) do think
   - (J) do not

5. **they're**
   - (A) they rest
   - (B) they are
   - (C) they run
   - (D) they care

6. **she'll**
   - (F) she falls
   - (G) she all
   - (H) she will
   - (J) she likes

STOP

READING: WORD ANALYSIS

● **Lesson 6: Root Words and Suffixes**

Directions: Choose the best answer to each question.

Examples

A. Which word is the root or base word for the word **mostly**?

- Ⓐ cost
- Ⓑ tly
- Ⓒ ly
- Ⓓ most

B. Which word is the ending or suffix for the word **helpless**?

- Ⓕ elp
- Ⓖ help
- Ⓗ less
- Ⓙ ess

 **Clue** Stay with your first answer. Change it only if you are sure it is wrong and another answer is better.

● **Practice**

1. Which word is the root word for **kindness**?
   - Ⓐ in
   - Ⓑ ness
   - Ⓒ kind
   - Ⓓ ind

2. Which word is the root word for **trying**?
   - Ⓕ try
   - Ⓖ ing
   - Ⓗ rying
   - Ⓙ tri

3. Which word is the root word for **faster**?
   - Ⓐ fas
   - Ⓑ fast
   - Ⓒ aster
   - Ⓓ ter

4. Which word is the suffix for **rested**?
   - Ⓕ ted
   - Ⓖ rest
   - Ⓗ ed
   - Ⓙ sted

5. Which word is the suffix for **softly**?
   - Ⓐ ftly
   - Ⓑ soft
   - Ⓒ sof
   - Ⓓ ly

6. Which word is the suffix for **treatment**?
   - Ⓕ treat
   - Ⓖ eat
   - Ⓗ ment
   - Ⓙ nt

STOP

Name _____   Date _____

READING: WORD ANALYSIS
SAMPLE TEST

● **Directions:** Choose the best answer to each question.

A. **Which word has the same beginning sound as cheese?**

   Ⓐ shoe

   Ⓑ chick

   Ⓒ clip

   Ⓓ sleep

---

1. **Which word has the same ending sound as lamp?**

   Ⓐ mad

   Ⓑ stomp

   Ⓒ lamb

   Ⓓ best

2. **Which word has the same vowel sound as plane?**

   Ⓕ stain

   Ⓖ than

   Ⓗ stand

   Ⓙ many

3. **Which word has the same ending sound as build?**

   Ⓐ bell

   Ⓑ cold

   Ⓒ heart

   Ⓓ bring

4. **Which word has the same vowel sound as bead?**

   Ⓕ round

   Ⓖ rest

   Ⓗ meet

   Ⓙ does

5. **Which word has the same ending sound as best?**

   Ⓐ loss

   Ⓑ most

   Ⓒ mess

   Ⓓ told

6. **Which word has the same beginning sound as straw?**

   Ⓕ try

   Ⓖ strike

   Ⓗ rain

   Ⓙ gone

GO ON

READING: WORD ANALYSIS
SAMPLE TEST

● **Directions:** Choose the best answer to each question.

Example

B. Which picture rhymes with the
    word **more**?

 (F)

 (G)

(H)

7. Which picture rhymes with the word **far**?

(A)

(B)

(C)

8. Which picture rhymes with the word **rain**?

(F)

(G)

(H)

9. Which picture rhymes with the word **dragon**?

(A)

(B)

(C)

10. Which picture rhymes with the word **soon**?

(F)

(G)

(H)

GO ON →

18

Name _____ Date_____

● **Directions:** Choose the best answer to each question.

Examples

C. Which word is a compound word, a word that is made up of two smaller words?

- (A) started
- (B) haircut
- (C) stand
- (D) tried

D. Look at the word. Find the answer that tells what the contraction means.
let's

- (F) let sister
- (G) let see
- (H) let us
- (J) let go

---

11. Which word is a compound word?

- (A) someday
- (B) dinner
- (C) jumping
- (D) second

12. Which word is a compound word?

- (F) simple
- (G) probably
- (H) however
- (J) going

13. Which word is a compound word?

- (A) summer
- (B) turned
- (C) trouble
- (D) bedroom

14. isn't

- (F) is now
- (G) is not
- (H) is thinking
- (J) is nose

15. you're

- (A) you read
- (B) you eat
- (C) you are
- (D) you is

16. they'll

- (F) they ball
- (G) they like
- (H) they leave
- (J) they will

GO ON

READING: WORD ANALYSIS
SAMPLE TEST

● **Directions:** Choose the best answer to each question.

Examples

E. Which word is the root or base word for the word **dreaming**?	**F.** Which word is the ending or suffix for the word **brighter**?
(A) ing	(F) ight
(B) eam	(G) er
(C) aming	(H) bright
(D) dream	(J) ghter

17. Which word is the root word for **calling**?

(A) ing
(B) call
(C) all
(D) alling

18. Which word is the root word for **sadness**?

(F) sad
(G) ness
(H) adness
(J) bad

19. Which word is the root word for **asked**?

(A) mask
(B) ed
(C) ked
(D) ask

20. Which word is the suffix for **darkly**?

(F) ly
(G) dark
(H) arkly
(J) door

21. Which word is the suffix for **helpful**?

(A) help
(B) ful
(C) elpful
(D) pful

22. Which word is the suffix for **picked**?

(F) pick
(G) sick
(H) icked
(J) ed

STOP

Name _____   Date_____

● **Lesson 7: Picture Vocabulary**

Directions: Choose the word that matches the picture.

_____ Examples _____

A. This one has been done for you.	**B.** Practice this one with your teacher.

A.
- Ⓐ bottle
- Ⓑ pour
- Ⓒ glass
- Ⓓ spill

B.
- Ⓕ sleep
- Ⓖ baby
- Ⓗ blanket
- Ⓙ awake

 Clue Look at the picture carefully and then read the choices.

● **Practice**

1.

- Ⓐ clean
- Ⓑ sing
- Ⓒ blow
- Ⓓ eat

3.

- Ⓐ baby
- Ⓑ stand
- Ⓒ come
- Ⓓ crib

2.

- Ⓕ crying
- Ⓖ happy
- Ⓗ smiling
- Ⓙ talking

4.

- Ⓕ out
- Ⓖ whisper
- Ⓗ shout
- Ⓙ laugh

STOP

READING: VOCABULARY

● **Lesson 8: Word Meaning**

Directions: Look at the underlined words in each sentence. Which word means the same thing?

Example

A. **Which word is part of your hand?**

    Ⓐ toe

    Ⓑ tooth

    Ⓒ ring

    Ⓓ finger

 Clue Key words in the question will help you find the answer.

● **Practice**

1. **Which word is something that flies?**

    Ⓐ bird

    Ⓑ cat

    Ⓒ worm

    Ⓓ dog

2. **Which word means to leave?**

    Ⓕ enter

    Ⓖ grow

    Ⓗ exit

    Ⓙ stay

3. **Which word means to finish?**

    Ⓐ finally

    Ⓑ different

    Ⓒ start

    Ⓓ complete

4. **Which word means to start?**

    Ⓕ read

    Ⓖ begin

    Ⓗ end

    Ⓙ done

5. **Which word is something you drive on?**

    Ⓐ shoes

    Ⓑ road

    Ⓒ stop

    Ⓓ door

6. **Which word is where a worm lives?**

    Ⓕ ground

    Ⓖ nest

    Ⓗ house

    Ⓙ car

STOP

READING: VOCABULARY

● **Lesson 9: Synonyms**

Directions: Look at the underlined word in each sentence. Which word is a synonym for that word?

Example

A. His clothes were <u>muddy</u>.

  Ⓐ loose
  Ⓑ cheap
  Ⓒ baggy
  Ⓓ dirty

 Clue Use other words in the sentence to help you find the meaning of the word.

● **Practice**

1. **Jesse wanted to solve the hard <u>riddle</u>.**

  Ⓐ job
  Ⓑ race
  Ⓒ puzzle
  Ⓓ portion

2. **Carol thought it was a <u>strange</u> day.**

  Ⓕ nice
  Ⓖ long
  Ⓗ short
  Ⓙ different

3. **Alyson was <u>always</u> smiling.**

  Ⓐ never
  Ⓑ forever
  Ⓒ usually
  Ⓓ sometimes

4. **They like to <u>create</u> jokes.**

  Ⓕ make
  Ⓖ bake
  Ⓗ hear
  Ⓙ doing

5. **He likes to eat <u>small</u> apples.**

  Ⓐ little
  Ⓑ rain
  Ⓒ ready
  Ⓓ leave

6. **She <u>watched</u> as the sun came up.**

  Ⓕ licked
  Ⓖ heard
  Ⓗ felt
  Ⓙ looked

STOP

READING: VOCABULARY

● **Lesson 10: Antonyms**

Directions: Look at the underlined word in each sentence. Choose the word that is the antonym of the underlined word.

Example

A. His room was <u>large</u>.

   Ⓐ pretty

   Ⓑ big

   Ⓒ small

   Ⓓ noisy

 Clue Look for the answer that means the opposite of the underlined word. Skip difficult questions and come back to them later.

● **Practice**

1. Her brother was <u>young</u>.

   Ⓐ busy

   Ⓑ new

   Ⓒ tired

   Ⓓ old

2. The family took a trip to the <u>city</u>.

   Ⓕ zoo

   Ⓖ park

   Ⓗ country

   Ⓙ building

3. The bedroom was always <u>messy</u>.

   Ⓐ lost

   Ⓑ neat

   Ⓒ sand

   Ⓓ dirty

4. She was the <u>best</u> at spelling.

   Ⓕ worst

   Ⓖ simple

   Ⓗ good

   Ⓙ rest

5. They had <u>real</u> money to go shopping.

   Ⓐ need

   Ⓑ less

   Ⓒ fake

   Ⓓ his

6. My <u>sister</u> likes ice cream.

   Ⓕ mother

   Ⓖ father

   Ⓗ brother

   Ⓙ uncle

STOP

READING: VOCABULARY

● **Lesson 11: Words in Context**

Directions: Choose the word that best fits in the blank.

Examples

The ____**(A)**____ was easy to enter. All you had to do was go to the park.
To win, you had to ____**(B)**____ how many jelly beans were in the jar.

A.
- Ⓐ door
- Ⓑ contest
- Ⓒ tunnel

B.
- Ⓕ guess
- Ⓖ read
- Ⓗ count

Clue When deciding which answer is best, try each answer choice in the blank.

● **Practice**

Each house on the block had a
____**(1)**____ backyard. Each had small
patches of lawn and flowers. Some
even had____**(2)**____ gardens.

1.
- Ⓐ unlikely
- Ⓑ neat
- Ⓒ lost

2.
- Ⓕ sand
- Ⓖ problem
- Ⓗ vegetable

One morning Chris couldn't
____**(3)**____ his homework. He looked
on his ____**(4)**____, but it wasn't there.
He wondered, "Where could it be?"

3.
- Ⓐ find
- Ⓑ hidden
- Ⓒ hear

4.
- Ⓕ lamp
- Ⓖ dog
- Ⓗ desk

STOP

READING: VOCABULARY

● **Lesson 12: Multiple Meaning Words**

Directions: Some words have more than one meaning. Choose the word that will make sense in both blanks.

Example

A. I _____ for the door.
She bumped her _____ when she fell.

- (A) went
- (B) leg
- (C) self
- (D) head

Clue Remember, the correct answer must make sense in both blanks.

● **Practice**

1. _____ the light over here.
The _____ on this pencil broke.

- (A) point
- (B) eraser
- (C) shine
- (D) top

2. The boat began to _____.
Dad washed the dishes in the _____.

- (F) wait
- (G) tub
- (H) sink
- (J) pan

3. Hit the _____ with the hammer.
The _____ on my little finger is broken.

- (A) tack
- (B) nail
- (C) skin
- (D) wood

4. Did you _____ your visitor well?
My dog loves to get a _____ from me.

- (F) feed
- (G) snack
- (H) enjoy
- (J) treat

5. The brown _____ was sleeping in the cave.
She could not _____ to hear any more scary stories.

- (A) hear
- (B) fox
- (C) bear
- (D) take

STOP

READING: VOCABULARY
SAMPLE TEST

● **Directions:** Choose the action word that best matches the picture.

Example

A.

- Ⓐ drop
- Ⓑ help
- Ⓒ climb
- Ⓓ slide

Look at the picture carefully and then read the choices.

1.

- Ⓐ mix
- Ⓑ fix
- Ⓒ eat
- Ⓓ chew

3.

- Ⓐ drink
- Ⓑ glass
- Ⓒ milk
- Ⓓ spill

2.

- Ⓕ lake
- Ⓖ boil
- Ⓗ bake
- Ⓙ lick

4.

- Ⓕ hug
- Ⓖ laugh
- Ⓗ tug
- Ⓙ cook

GO ON

Name _____   Date _____

READING: VOCABULARY

SAMPLE TEST

● **Directions:** Look at the underlined words in each sentence. Which word means the same thing?

Example

B.   **Which word means <u>being with others</u>?**

    (F)   alone

    (G)   many

    (H)   together

    (J)   busy

Key words in the question will help you find the answer.

5.   **Which word is <u>to lift up</u>?**

    (A)   find

    (B)   raise

    (C)   release

    (D)   haul

6.   **Which word means <u>to be quick</u>?**

    (F)   slow

    (G)   fast

    (H)   walk

    (J)   run

7.   **Which word means <u>to drop down</u>?**

    (A)   fall

    (B)   lift

    (C)   wish

    (D)   see

8.   **Which word is <u>part of a tree</u>?**

    (F)   shade

    (G)   cool

    (H)   leaf

    (J)   moist

9.   **Which word is <u>something cold</u>?**

    (A)   short

    (B)   small

    (C)   fire

    (D)   ice

10.   **Which word is <u>part of a flower</u>?**

    (F)   petal

    (G)   dirt

    (H)   bee

    (J)   pot

GO ON

1-57768-722-1 *Spectrum Test Practice 2*

READING: VOCABULARY
SAMPLE TEST

Examples

Look at the underlined word in each sentence. Which word is a synonym for that word?

C. She was <u>certain</u> she would be able to fix the broken clock.

- (A) loose
- (B) sure
- (C) baggy
- (D) dirty

Look at the underlined word in each sentence. Which word is an antonym for that word?

D. He was very <u>nervous</u> to talk in front of the class.

- (F) calm
- (G) annoyed
- (H) frightened
- (J) excited

---

11. Flossie <u>actually</u> knew a lot about social studies.

- (A) rarely
- (B) really
- (C) seldom
- (D) never

12. Jack found a giant rock to add to his <u>rock</u> garden.

- (F) sand
- (G) stone
- (H) marble
- (J) apple

13. She knew where the <u>hidden</u> key was kept.

- (A) open
- (B) known
- (C) friendly
- (D) secret

14. The plane was going to fly very <u>high</u>.

- (F) low
- (G) land
- (H) middle
- (J) people

15. Alan's doctor said he was <u>healthy</u>.

- (A) wound
- (B) heal
- (C) sick
- (D) find

16. She was always <u>early</u> to school.

- (F) help
- (G) late
- (H) same
- (J) funny

GO ON

READING: VOCABULARY
SAMPLE TEST

● **Directions:** Choose the word that best fits in the blanks.

Examples

Beth watched the rain _____**(E)**_____ down the window. Rain meant no picnic in the park with Grandma. Beth liked going to the park because it had _____**(F)**_____ birds and a swing set.

E.
- (A) jump
- (B) walk
- (C) slide

F.
- (F) laughing
- (G) singing
- (H) crying

When deciding which answer is best, try each answer choice in the blank.

Matt and Alan _____**(17)**_____ with their kites to the top of the high hill. They laid down in the _____**(18)**_____ grass and watched the clouds.

17.
- (A) raced
- (B) picked
- (C) took

18.
- (F) stop
- (G) winter
- (H) soft

Alicia and her brother Randy hurried out the _____**(19)**_____ in their heavy snowsuits. They played in the snow. They made a big snowman in the _____**(20)**_____.

19.
- (A) door
- (B) window
- (C) space

20.
- (F) backyard
- (G) sand
- (H) garage

Name _____   Date _____

READING: COMPREHENSION

● **Lesson 13: Picture Comprehension**

Directions: Look at the picture. Then choose the word that best fits in the blank.

Example

A. **The train is _____ in a few minutes.**

  (A) whistled
  (B) arriving
  (C) hours
  (D) floating

 Clue Look back at the picture when you choose an answer to fit in the blank.

● **Practice**

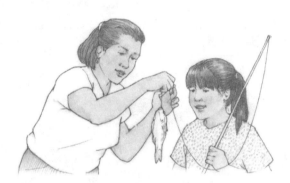

1. **The line for the movie _____ around the corner.**

  (A) went
  (B) ran
  (C) skipped
  (D) sang

3. **Jenna caught small fish on her new fishing _____.**

  (A) bait
  (B) camp
  (C) box
  (D) rod

2. **This was a film that everyone wanted to _____.**

  (F) like
  (G) hear
  (H) see
  (J) drink

4. **Her _____ helped her take it off the hook.**

  (F) mom
  (G) dad
  (H) baby
  (J) brother

 STOP

READING: COMPREHENSION

● **Lesson 14: Critical Reading**

Directions: Read each sentence. Choose the sentence that describes something that could **not** happen.

Example

A. Ⓐ The wind was blowing hard and it was snowing.

Ⓑ Because of the storm, school was closed.

Ⓒ Pedro and Juanita dressed in warm clothing to play outside.

Ⓓ Their dog, Barney, dressed himself in a hat and gloves too.

 Clue Read the sentences carefully. Think about what could and could not happen.

● **Practice**

1. Ⓐ Mr. and Mrs. Jennings heard a noise outside and realized their kitten was missing.

Ⓑ Mrs. Jennings flapped her arms fast and flew out the door.

Ⓒ They looked under the bushes and all around the house.

Ⓓ They weren't sure where the kitten was hiding but they kept looking.

2. Ⓕ Uncle Paul and Jeff were sailing their boat.

Ⓖ It was windy and they were having a good day.

Ⓗ It was almost time for lunch.

Ⓙ Out of the clouds dropped a picnic basket filled with food.

STOP

Name _____   Date_____

● **Lesson 15: Fiction**

Directions: Read or listen to the story below and answer the questions that follow.

Example

Camels are strong, sturdy animals that live in the desert. Camels are able to live in the desert because their bodies are designed for it.

A. **What is the main idea?**
- (A) camels are strong animals
- (B) living in the desert
- (C) bodies
- (D) animals in the desert

● **Practice** **Read or listen to the paragraph below. It tells about a girl who thinks it would be great if no one could see her. Then answer the questions.**

If Cassie Was Invisible

Cassie kicked at the dirty clothes on her floor. She was upset. Her dad told her to clean her room. Cassie wished she was invisible. Then she wouldn't have to clean anything! If she was invisible, she would go to school and not do any work. She would stay up late. She would never have to take baths. Best of all, her brother couldn't pick on her. But, wait! If she was invisible, she wouldn't get any apple pie. And no one would ask her to play. Cassie would never get to hug her grandparents. Maybe being invisible wouldn't be so much fun after all.

1. **In the beginning, why does Cassie want to be invisible?**
- (A) Because she wants to play.
- (B) Because she loves apple pie.
- (C) Because she didn't like dad.
- (D) Because she didn't want to clean her room.

2. **Why does Cassie decide she doesn't want to be invisible?**
- (F) She loves to clean.
- (G) Her mom misses her.
- (H) She wouldn't get to hug her grandparents.
- (J) She wants to be smart.

3. **Who is the main character in the story?**
- (A) the dad
- (B) Cassie
- (C) the grandparents
- (D) the teacher

4. **Where does the story take place?**
- (F) at school
- (G) at Cassie's grandparents
- (H) at the park
- (J) at Cassie's house

GO ON

● **Lesson 15: Fiction (cont.)**

Directions: Read or listen to the story below. It tells about Sam being the oldest child in his family. Then answer the questions.

The Oldest

Sometimes, Sam likes being the oldest. He can stay up one hour later. He can go places by himself. He also gets a bigger allowance for helping around the house. When his friend Brennan asks him to spend the night, Sam's mom says yes. He even gets to stay at his friend's house to eat dinner sometimes. Sam thinks it's great that he can read, ride a bike, and spell better than his brother. Sam's sister loves when he reads stories to her. Sam likes it too. When his mom needs help cooking, she asks Sam because he is the oldest.

Sometimes, Sam doesn't like being the oldest. He has to babysit his sister. She likes to go where he does. He also has to act more like a grown-up. Sam always has more jobs to do around the house. He has to help wash the dishes and take out the trash. His brother and sister get help when they have to clean their rooms. Sam doesn't get help. Sam doesn't like to be the oldest when his brother and sister want him to play with them all the time.

5. **What can Sam do better than his brother?**

   Ⓐ play soccer

   Ⓑ eat candy

   Ⓒ ride a bike

   Ⓓ watch movies

6. **What does Sam think about having to act more like a grown-up?**

   Ⓕ He likes it.

   Ⓖ He thinks his brother should act more grown-up.

   Ⓗ It is one reason why he doesn't like to be the oldest.

   Ⓙ He wants his parents to treat his brother like they treat him.

7. **Who is the main character in the story?**

   Ⓐ Brennan

   Ⓑ the sister

   Ⓒ the brother

   Ⓓ Sam

8. **What is the main idea of the story?**

   Ⓕ washing dishes

   Ⓖ eating dinner

   Ⓗ playing outside

   Ⓙ being the oldest

READING: COMPREHENSION

● **Lesson 16: Nonfiction**

Directions: Read or listen to the paragraph below that tells how to make a peanut butter and jelly sandwich. Then answer the questions.

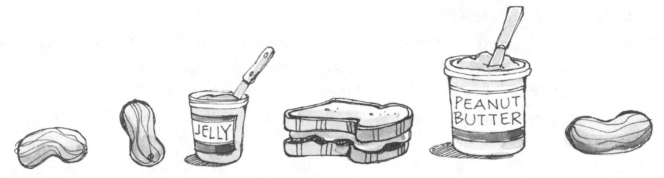

How to Make a Peanut Butter and Jelly Sandwich

You will need peanut butter, jelly, and two pieces of bread. First, spread peanut butter on one piece of bread. Next, spread jelly on the other piece. Then, put the two pieces of bread together. Next, cut the sandwich in half. Last, eat your sandwich and enjoy!

1. **What is the paragraph explaining?**
   - Ⓐ how to make peanut butter
   - Ⓑ how to cut sandwiches
   - Ⓒ how to make peanut butter and jelly sandwiches
   - Ⓓ how to put bread together

2. **Which of these is an opinion?**
   - Ⓕ Peanut butter and jelly sandwiches have jelly in them.
   - Ⓖ The paragraph says to cut the sandwich.
   - Ⓗ You can use two pieces of bread.
   - Ⓙ Peanut butter and jelly sandwiches are great.

3. **What does the paragraph say to do after you spread peanut butter on one piece of bread?**
   - Ⓐ cut the sandwich
   - Ⓑ spread jelly on the other piece of bread
   - Ⓒ put the two pieces together
   - Ⓓ eat your sandwich and enjoy eating it

4. **What don't you need to make a peanut butter and jelly sandwich?**
   - Ⓕ bread
   - Ⓖ peanut butter
   - Ⓗ milk
   - Ⓙ jelly

READING: COMPREHENSION

● Lesson 16: Nonfiction (cont.)

Directions: Read or listen to the paragraph below that tells about dolphins and sharks. Then answer the questions.

Dolphins and Sharks

Dolphins and sharks both live in the ocean, but they are very different. Dolphins are mammals. Sharks are fish. Both animals swim underwater. Sharks breathe through gills, and dolphins have lungs. Dolphins breathe through a blowhole on their heads. Dolphins have smooth, slippery skin, but sharks have scales. Dolphins give birth to live young. Sharks lay eggs. When the eggs hatch, young sharks come out. Sharks and dolphins live in water, but they have many differences.

5. **Which animal has smooth, slippery skin?**

   (A) dolphins

   (B) sharks

   (C) eggs

   (D) fish

6. **Why did the author write about dolphins and sharks?**

   (F) to feel the smooth skin of the dolphins

   (G) to learn how to swim

   (H) to tell others about dolphins and sharks

   (J) to breathe through the gills

7. **What do you know about dolphins and sharks?**

   (A) They are mostly alike.

   (B) They both have blowholes.

   (C) There are many different things about them.

   (D) They live in rivers and streams.

8. **What do sharks need to breathe?**

   (F) lungs

   (G) blowholes

   (H) noses

   (J) gills

STOP

Name _____ Date _____

● **Directions:** Read or listen to the story below. Then answer the questions. The story is about two boys who are best friends.

Example

Best Friends

In second grade, Chad and Ryan were best friends. Both boys loved all kinds of sports. In the spring, they played baseball.

A. What is a fact about Chad and Ryan?

- (A) They were best friends.
- (B) They did not like sports.
- (C) Playing outside is not allowed.
- (D) They always wore socks when taking a bath.

During the summer, Chad and Ryan enjoyed swimming and street hockey. Chad swam on a swim team. Ryan went to meets so he could cheer for Chad. In the fall, the boys played pee-wee football. They won most of their games and made several new friends. During the winter months, both boys played basketball. Ryan also played on a weekend ice-hockey team. Chad went to the games so he could yell for Ryan and his team. The two boys decided to call themselves "Best Sports Pals" and stay friends forever.

1. What does the phrase "cheer for Chad" mean?

- (A) to play football
- (B) to yell for Chad to do a good job
- (C) to scream for Chad to make a mistake
- (D) to listen carefully to your parents

2. What sport do the boys play in the fall?

- (F) football
- (G) basketball
- (H) hockey
- (J) baseball

3. What is another title for the story?

- (A) Hockey Is Fun
- (B) Play Football!
- (C) Friends That Always Win
- (D) Best Sports Pals

4. What do you think Chad would do if Ryan decided to play soccer and baseball in the spring?

- (F) Chad would never go see Ryan play a game.
- (G) Chad would cry.
- (H) Chad would quit playing.
- (J) Chad would make sure to go to see Ryan play soccer.

GO ON

READING: COMPREHENSION
SAMPLE TEST

● **Directions:** Read or listen to the story below. Then answer the questions. The story is about a new boy named Raj who is deaf and comes to Patsy's school. Raj was born in India, and he knows sign language, English, and Hindi, his family's language in India. The story tells about Patsy's first experience with Raj.

A New Friend

"Can I sit here?" asked Raj in an unusual voice. He signed while he talked, and it was a little difficult to understand him.

"Sure," answered Patsy. She was very nervous, and her words barely came out. "What am I supposed to do?" she asked herself. "I've never met a deaf person before."

All that morning, Patsy kept looking over at Raj. He seemed to be able to understand what was going on in class. "How does he do that?" she wondered to herself. That afternoon, Mrs. Martin took some time to let Raj and the other students get to know each other better. Patsy was surprised to find that her friend, Kyle, actually knew sign language. Soon, Patsy found she could understand most of what Raj was saying.

That afternoon, Raj and Patsy walked home together. Patsy learned some signs and told Raj about her family. By the time they reached Raj's house, she was able to sign "good-bye."

5. **What do you think about Raj from reading the story?**
   - Ⓐ He is embarrassed.
   - Ⓑ He is pleasant.
   - Ⓒ He is unfriendly.
   - Ⓓ He is very tall.

6. **What do you think Patsy will do in a few weeks?**
   - Ⓕ She will forget sign language.
   - Ⓖ She won't walk home with Raj.
   - Ⓗ She will look for other friends.
   - Ⓙ She will have learned more sign language.

7. **What would you conclude from reading this story?**
   - Ⓐ Raj makes new friends easily.
   - Ⓑ Raj has a hard time learning languages.
   - Ⓒ Raj was more frightened than Patsy.
   - Ⓓ Raj was not a nice person.

8. **Which of the following is a fact?**
   - Ⓕ Patsy isn't a nice girl.
   - Ⓖ Patsy will never learn sign language.
   - Ⓗ Raj knows sign language.
   - Ⓙ Raj and Patsy will become best friends.

GO ON

Name _____ Date _____

● **Directions:** Read or listen to the paragraphs about how people talk in the country of India. Then answer the questions. India is a country near China. Much like the U.S.A. is next to Canada, India is next to China. Have you ever heard of the country of India?

India

In the U.S.A. most people speak English. In India, there are over 1,000 different languages. This has caused many problems. Many of the people speak the words in different ways. Hindi was made the main language to speak to solve the problem. However, it is still hard for people to talk to each other.

There are many ways to let others know what you think without words. Some actions mean different things in India. For example, to show an older person that you respect him, bow down and touch his feet. If you want to be rude, sit with the bottoms of your shoes showing. To show you are clean, never wear your shoes in the house or in the kitchen. If you don't want to be polite, point at your feet.

9. **What can you do to be rude in India?**
   - (A) Never wear your shoes in the house.
   - (B) Learn how to read.
   - (C) Sit with the bottoms of your shoes showing.
   - (D) Go to the store.

10. **What is the main idea of the paragraphs?**
    - (F) It is fun to live in India.
    - (G) Learning to read is important.
    - (H) Never point at your feet or show the bottom of your shoes.
    - (J) There are many ways to let others know what you think in India.

11. **What do you think people feel about talking to each other In India?**
    - (A) It is easy to talk to others.
    - (B) It is mostly easy to talk to others.
    - (C) It is hard to talk to others.
    - (D) It is just like in the U.S.A.

12. **What can you do to show respect in India?**
    - (F) Wear your socks outside.
    - (G) Bow down and touch an older person's feet.
    - (H) Frown at people.
    - (J) Talk quietly.

GO ON

Name _____ Date_____

● **Directions:** Read or listen to the paragraphs below about sign language.
Then answer the questions.

Sign Language

People who may not be able to hear or speak well use sign language. They use their hands instead of their voices to talk. Their hands make signals to show different letters, words, and ideas. For example, to say the word "love," cross your arms over your chest.

Other people use sign language too. Have you ever watched a football game? The referees use hand signals to let you know what has happened in the game, such as a foul or time out. Have you ever been stuck in a traffic jam where there is a police officer? The police can use sign language to tell cars to go and wait.

Guess who else uses sign language? You! You wave your hand when you say hello and good-bye. You nod your head up and down to say "yes" and back and forth to say "no." You use your fingers to point and show which way to go. We use our hands and body to make signals all of the time!

13. **Why do people use sign language?**
   - (A) Because they don't feel like talking.
   - (B) Because they don't feel like listening.
   - (C) Because they cannot ride a bike.
   - (D) Because they cannot hear or speak well.

14. **What do people use when signing?**
   - (F) their hand and arms
   - (G) their eyes, ears, and mouth
   - (H) their feet and legs
   - (J) their hair and head

15. **Who would be the most likely to use sign language?**
   - (A) a boy playing at the park
   - (B) a man who cannot hear
   - (C) a woman who cannot walk
   - (D) a girl learning to tie her shoe

16. **What is the main idea of the story?**
   - (F) using sign language
   - (G) writing sign language
   - (H) playing with children who use sign language
   - (J) buying food using sign language

STOP

ANSWER SHEET

Part 1: WORD ANALYSIS

A (A)(B)(C)(D)   5 (A)(B)(C)(D)   8 (F)(G)(H)(J)   D (F)(G)(H)   16 (F)(G)(H)   19 (A)(B)(C)(D)
1 (A)(B)(C)(D)   6 (F)(G)(H)(J)   9 (A)(B)(C)(D)   E (A)(B)(C)   F (F)(G)(H)(J)   20 (F)(G)(H)(J)
2 (F)(G)(H)(J)   B (F)(G)(H)(J)   10 (F)(G)(H)(J)   13 (A)(B)(C)   G (A)(B)(C)(D)   21 (A)(B)(C)(D)
3 (A)(B)(C)(D)   C (A)(B)(C)(D)   11 (A)(B)(C)(D)   14 (F)(G)(H)   17 (A)(B)(C)(D)   22 (F)(G)(H)(J)
4 (F)(G)(H)(J)   7 (A)(B)(C)(D)   12 (F)(G)(H)(J)   15 (A)(B)(C)   18 (F)(G)(H)

Part 2: VOCABULARY

A (A)(B)(C)(D)   6 (F)(G)(H)(J)   12 (F)(G)(H)(J)   18 (F)(G)(H)(J)   23 (A)(B)(C)(D)   29 (A)(B)(C)(D)
1 (A)(B)(C)(D)   7 (A)(B)(C)(D)   13 (A)(B)(C)(D)   19 (A)(B)(C)(D)   24 (F)(G)(H)(J)   30 (F)(G)(H)(J)
2 (F)(G)(H)(J)   8 (F)(G)(H)(J)   14 (F)(G)(H)(J)   20 (F)(G)(H)(J)   25 (A)(B)(C)(D)   31 (A)(B)(C)(D)
3 (A)(B)(C)(D)   9 (A)(B)(C)(D)   15 (A)(B)(C)(D)   21 (A)(B)(C)(D)   26 (F)(G)(H)(J)   32 (F)(G)(H)(J)
4 (F)(G)(H)(J)   10 (F)(G)(H)(J)   16 (F)(G)(H)(J)   22 (F)(G)(H)(J)   27 (A)(B)(C)(D)   33 (A)(B)(C)(D)
B (F)(G)(H)(J)   C (A)(B)(C)(D)   D (F)(G)(H)(J)   E (A)(B)(C)(D)   28 (F)(G)(H)(J)   34 (F)(G)(H)(J)
5 (A)(B)(C)(D)   11 (A)(B)(C)(D)   17 (A)(B)(C)(D)   F (F)(G)(H)(J)   G (A)(B)(C)(D)

Part 3: READING COMPREHENSION

A (A)(B)(C)(D)   4 (F)(G)(H)(J)   8 (F)(G)(H)(J)   12 (F)(G)(H)(J)   16 (F)(G)(H)(J)   20 (F)(G)(H)(J)
1 (A)(B)(C)(D)   5 (A)(B)(C)(D)   9 (A)(B)(C)(D)   13 (A)(B)(C)(D)   17 (A)(B)(C)(D)
2 (F)(G)(H)(J)   6 (F)(G)(H)(J)   10 (F)(G)(H)(J)   14 (F)(G)(H)(J)   18 (F)(G)(H)(J)
3 (A)(B)(C)(D)   7 (A)(B)(C)(D)   11 (A)(B)(C)(D)   15 (A)(B)(C)(D)   19 (A)(B)(C)(D)

Name _____   Date_____

● **Part 1: Word Analysis**

Directions: Choose the best answer to each question.

Example

A.   Which word has the same beginning sound as **small**?
  (A) snow
  (B) smooth
  (C) shown
  (D) something

1.   Which word has the same vowel sound as **catch**?
  (A) came
  (B) bad
  (C) eat
  (D) clean

2.   Which word has the same beginning sound as **block**?
  (F) box
  (G) breeze
  (H) blink
  (J) answer

3.   Which word has the same ending sound as **work**?
  (A) yard
  (B) stood
  (C) took
  (D) watch

4.   Which word has the same vowel sound as **stood**?
  (F) two
  (G) those
  (H) road
  (J) could

5.   Which word has the same ending sound as **with**?
  (A) while
  (B) kiss
  (C) bath
  (D) these

6.   Which word has the same beginning sound as **same**?
  (F) ham
  (G) rain
  (H) shall
  (J) sand

GO ON

1-57768-722-1 *Spectrum Test Practice 2*

READING PRACTICE TEST

● **Part 1: Word Analysis (cont.)**

Directions: Choose the best answer to each question.

Examples

B. **Which word is a compound word, a word that is made up of two smaller words?**

- (F) complete
- (G) certain
- (H) became
- (J) sunlight

C. **Look at the underlined word. Find the answer that tells what the contraction means.**
that'll

- (A) that is
- (B) that will
- (C) that all
- (D) that calls

If an item is too difficult, skip It and come back to it later.

7. **Which word is a compound word?**

- (A) sidewalk
- (B) building
- (C) darkness
- (D) small

8. **Which word is a compound word?**

- (F) several
- (G) party
- (H) person
- (J) playground

9. **Which word is a compound word?**

- (A) nice
- (B) clothes
- (C) snowball
- (D) picture

10. **needn't**

- (F) need noses
- (G) need not
- (H) need night
- (J) need next

11. **could've**

- (A) could leave
- (B) could have
- (C) could very
- (D) could has

12. **what's**

- (F) what is
- (G) what stinks
- (H) what shakes
- (J) what sees

GO ON

READING PRACTICE TEST

● **Part 1: Word Analysis (cont.)**

Directions: Choose the word that best fits in the blanks.

Examples

Jawan_____**(D)**_____ down at the table. He was
hungry and the _____**(E)**_____ looked good.

D.
- Ⓕ ate
- Ⓖ look
- Ⓗ sat

E.
- Ⓐ chair
- Ⓑ mom
- Ⓒ food

We usually take our vacation in July. Mom and Dad _____**(13)**_____ a house at the beach. It's not as big as our regular house, but everyone has a place to _____**(14)**_____.

It was my birthday! I was _____**(15)**_____ seven years old. My mom made me a pretty cake. I blew out all the candles. My mom and dad gave me a great gift, a _____**(16)**_____ bicycle!

13.
- Ⓐ rent
- Ⓑ park
- Ⓒ read

14.
- Ⓕ sand
- Ⓖ beach
- Ⓗ sleep

15.
- Ⓐ making
- Ⓑ turning
- Ⓒ looked

16.
- Ⓕ ugly
- Ⓖ new
- Ⓗ even

GO ON

44 1-57768-722-1 *Spectrum Test Practice 2*

READING PRACTICE TEST

● Part 1: Word Analysis (cont.)

Directions: Choose the best answer to each question.

Examples

F. Which word is the root or base word for the word **biggest**?

- (F) big
- (G) gest
- (H) est
- (J) bigge

G. Which word is the ending or suffix for the word **broken**?

- (A) en
- (B) broke
- (C) bro
- (D) roke

---

17. Which word is the root word for **certainly**?

- (A) ly
- (B) cert
- (C) certain
- (D) change

18. Which word is the root word for **fullness**?

- (F) falling
- (G) ness
- (H) full
- (J) fur

19. Which word is the root word for **slower**?

- (A) slip
- (B) er
- (C) low
- (D) slow

20. Which word is the suffix for **lighter**?

- (F) light
- (G) er
- (H) igh
- (J) lig

21. Which word is the suffix for **completely**?

- (A) ly
- (B) pete
- (C) complete
- (D) come

22. Which word is the suffix for **listing**?

- (F) ing
- (G) list
- (H) isti
- (J) licking

STOP

READING PRACTICE TEST

● Part 2: Vocabulary

Directions: Choose the word that best matches the picture.

Example

A.

- (A) hammer
- (B) drill
- (C) nail
- (D) wood

Look at the picture carefully and then read the choices.

1.

- (A) smell
- (B) feel
- (C) hear
- (D) see

3.

- (A) leaf
- (B) wood
- (C) branch
- (D) tree

2.

- (F) clap
- (G) shake
- (H) touch
- (J) snap

4.

- (F) watering
- (G) smoking
- (H) steaming
- (J) cooking

GO ON

READING PRACTICE TEST

● **Part 2: Vocabulary (cont.)**

Directions: Look at the underlined words in each sentence. Which word means the same thing?

> **Example**
>
> B.   **Which word means <u>to soar like a bird</u>?**
>
>   Ⓕ air
>
>   Ⓖ ride
>
>   Ⓗ run
>
>   Ⓙ fly
>
>

Key words in the question will help you find the answer.

5.   **Which word is <u>something that walks</u>?**

     Ⓐ cat

     Ⓑ worm

     Ⓒ snake

     Ⓓ fish

6.   **Which word means <u>to take air in through your nose</u>?**

     Ⓕ cough

     Ⓖ swim

     Ⓗ eat

     Ⓙ breathe

7.   **Which word means <u>to talk about</u>?**

     Ⓐ write

     Ⓑ dream

     Ⓒ enjoy

     Ⓓ discuss

8.   **Which word means <u>to follow after</u>?**

     Ⓕ chase

     Ⓖ begin

     Ⓗ fall

     Ⓙ turn

9.   **Which word means <u>feeling like you need something to eat</u>?**

     Ⓐ full

     Ⓑ hungry

     Ⓒ ate

     Ⓓ food

10.   **Which word means <u>to bend toward</u>?**

     Ⓕ lean

     Ⓖ reach

     Ⓗ sleep

     Ⓙ drop

GO ON

READING PRACTICE TEST

● **Part 2: Vocabulary (cont.)**

Directions: Look at the underlined word in each sentence. Which word is a synonym for that word?

Example

C. Her mom wrote a <u>note</u> to the teacher.

    Ⓐ message

    Ⓑ defeat

    Ⓒ pencil

    Ⓓ ticket

Use the meaning of the sentence to help you find the meaning of the word.

11. Susan was <u>grateful</u> that her dad drove her to <u>school</u>.

    Ⓐ thankful

    Ⓑ busy

    Ⓒ curious

    Ⓓ finished

12. The brothers <u>yelled</u> for their dog to come home.

    Ⓕ cared

    Ⓖ called

    Ⓗ heard

    Ⓙ whispered

13. Grandma asked me to <u>split</u> the cookies evenly between the children.

    Ⓐ use

    Ⓑ think

    Ⓒ divide

    Ⓓ stand

14. I always keep my room very <u>neat</u>.

    Ⓕ bad

    Ⓖ pretty

    Ⓗ tidy

    Ⓙ dark

15. She likes to eat <u>big</u> oranges.

    Ⓐ huge

    Ⓑ tiny

    Ⓒ ready

    Ⓓ round

16. She watched the cat <u>jump</u> off the chair.

    Ⓕ leap

    Ⓖ lick

    Ⓗ break

    Ⓙ dream

GO ON

READING PRACTICE TEST

● **Part 2: Vocabulary (cont.)**

Directions: Look at the underlined word in each sentence. Choose the word that is the antonym of the underlined word.

Example

D. He has an <u>unusual</u> voice.

- Ⓕ loud
- Ⓖ regular
- Ⓗ soft
- Ⓙ small

---

17. They drove down the <u>narrow</u> road.

- Ⓐ long
- Ⓑ new
- Ⓒ bumpy
- Ⓓ wide

18. She picked her <u>fancy</u> dress to wear to the party.

- Ⓕ best
- Ⓖ plain
- Ⓗ small
- Ⓙ little

19. She made sure the knot was good and <u>tight</u>.

- Ⓐ clean
- Ⓑ different
- Ⓒ loose
- Ⓓ last

20. After granting our three wishes, the kind fairy <u>vanished</u> from sight.

- Ⓕ appeared
- Ⓖ asked
- Ⓗ going
- Ⓙ got

21. He thought his bike was <u>fast</u>.

- Ⓐ funny
- Ⓑ food
- Ⓒ last
- Ⓓ slow

22. On Thursday, Daniel was <u>absent</u>.

- Ⓕ giving
- Ⓖ present
- Ⓗ hurt
- Ⓙ gone

GO ON

═══ READING PRACTICE TEST ═══

● **Part 2: Vocabulary (cont.)**

Directions: Choose the word that best fits in the blanks.

Examples

Mr. Jennings went _____**(E)**_____ after work. He bought food
for dinner and then he went _____**(F)**_____.

E.
- (A) shopping
- (B) walking
- (C) driving

F.
- (F) soon
- (G) fast
- (H) home

When deciding which answer is best, try each answer choice in the blank.

Our neighbor is a gardener. One of
her _____**(23)**_____ trees recently died. She
said it was because of a bug that likes
to eat _____**(24)**_____.

23.
- (A) girl
- (B) half
- (C) small

24.
- (F) each
- (G) leaves
- (H) dirt

One sunny June day, a man
_____**(25)**_____ too fast down the road. A
police officer stopped him and gave him
a _____**(26)**_____.

25.
- (A) drove
- (B) paced
- (C) ran

26.
- (F) picture
- (G) ticket
- (H) rest

27. There are many different
_____**(27)**_____ **of bats. One kind is**
the brown bat.
- (A) only
- (B) paper
- (C) kinds

28. _____**(28)**_____ **brown bats eat**
insects. One bat can eat 600
mosquitoes in just an hour.
- (F) second
- (G) little
- (H) sleep

GO ON

READING PRACTICE TEST

● **Part 2: Vocabulary (cont.)**

Directions: Some words have more than one meaning. Choose the word that will make sense in both blanks.

Example

G. My mom gets to take _____ at work.
I get mad when my brother _____ my toys.

- (A) misses
- (B) breaks
- (C) picks
- (D) walks

29. He carried his _____ to the baseball field.
The _____ was hanging in the cave.

- (A) bat
- (B) men
- (C) ball
- (D) sheep

30. In the _____ my mom plants all of her flowers.
The _____ next to the mountain had fresh water.

- (F) picnic
- (G) fall
- (H) spring
- (J) snow

31. Did you go to the _____ with your friends?
Where should I _____ the car?

- (A) party
- (B) school
- (C) park
- (D) drive

32. A bear has a heavy _____.
My mom bought me a new _____ for winter.

- (F) hat
- (G) fur
- (H) enjoy
- (J) coat

33. The river _____ into two separate streams.
The _____ on the tree swayed in the wind.

- (A) leaves
- (B) branches
- (C) wanted
- (D) goes

34. Cinderella was the most beautiful girl at the _____.
Hunter's grandma bought him a red _____ for his birthday.

- (F) party
- (G) gift
- (H) ball
- (J) bike

STOP

Name _____   Date_____

READING PRACTICE TEST

● **Part 3: Story Comprehension**

<table>
<tr>
<td>

Example

Bigfoot is a creature that may be real or make-believe. Although many people say they have seen this creature, scientists want more proof. Is there a man-like beast lurking around the woods in countries all over the world?

</td>
<td>

A. What is Bigfoot?

Ⓐ a huge foot

Ⓑ a giant sock

Ⓒ a creature

Ⓓ a country

</td>
</tr>
</table>

Read or listen to the paragraph below that tells about horses. Then answer the questions.

Horses

Horses are beautiful animals. Most horses have smooth, shiny coats. They have long manes and tails. Their hair may be brown, black, white, yellow, or spotted. Sometimes horses neigh, or make a loud, long cry. Horses need to be brushed every day. This helps keep them clean. Many people keep horses as pets or to work on farms. Some people enjoy riding them for fun. Horses are wonderful animals.

1. **What does the word neigh mean?**

Ⓐ to smile

Ⓑ to be different colors

Ⓒ to keep clean by brushing

Ⓓ to make a loud, long cry

2. **How often should horses be brushed?**

Ⓕ every day

Ⓖ every week

Ⓗ every month

Ⓙ every year

3. **What do you know about horses?**

Ⓐ Horses are the same color.

Ⓑ Horses never make noise.

Ⓒ Some people enjoy riding horses for fun.

Ⓓ Horses have feathers.

4. **If you had a horse for a pet, what might happen?**

Ⓕ You would have to feed it.

Ⓖ You would have to brush its mane and tail.

Ⓗ You would have to have a place for the horse to stay.

Ⓙ All of the above

GO ON ⇨

READING PRACTICE TEST

● Part 3: Story Comprehension (cont.)

Directions: Read or listen to the paragraphs below that tells about stars. Then answer the questions.

Stars

(1) When you look up on a clear, dark night, you can see small points of light called stars. Actually, stars are not small at all. Some stars may be 50 million miles across! Stars just look like points of light because they are so far from Earth. Our sun is a star. It looks bigger than other stars in the sky because it is closer to us. A star's brightness depends on its mass and distance from Earth. Bigger stars are brighter than smaller ones. Stars also look brighter when they are closer.

(2) To make it easier to study, people have grouped stars into patterns. The patterns are called constellations. They may be large or small. They may have bright or dim stars. Sometimes in a constellation, the bright stars may be in the shape of a person or animal.

(3) Stars, unlike planets, make their own heat and light. The color of a star's light can tell us how much heat it has. The cooler stars give off a reddish light. The hottest stars look blue or blue-white in color. Stars do not last the same amount of time. They all will eventually burn out.

5. **What does the word constellation mean?**
   - (A) large and in space
   - (B) different stars people see from Mars
   - (C) different color stars we can see from the earth
   - (D) a pattern of stars that are grouped together

6. **Which of the following is an opinion?**
   - (F) Stars are fun to look at every night.
   - (G) Our sun is a star.
   - (H) Stars look brighter when they are closer.
   - (J) Cooler stars give off a reddish light.

7. **What is a supporting detail for paragraph 2?**
   - (A) Colors of stars help us to know how hot they are.
   - (B) Our sun is a star.
   - (C) It takes imagination to find when different patterns in the sky look like people or animals.
   - (D) When stars burn out they turn into new kinds of stars.

8. **What would happen if you traveled through space and got closer and closer to a star?**
   - (F) You would see it get smaller.
   - (G) It would look like a rainbow.
   - (H) It would get brighter.
   - (J) All of the above

GO ON

READING PRACTICE TEST

● **Part 3: Story Comprehension (cont.)**

Directions: Read or listen to the paragraph below. It tells about honey and bees. Then answer the questions.

Sweet as Honey

Honey is sweet and thick. Honeybees make it. First, they fly from flower to flower. At each flower, they collect nectar. Nectar is watery. It is found inside flower blossoms. The bees sip the nectar from flowers. Next, they store it in their bodies. It is kept in their honey bags. Then, the nectar in the honey bags changes. It changes into two kinds of sugars. The bees fly back to their hives. Finally, they put the nectar into their hives. While it is there, most of the water leaves or evaporates. All that is left is the sweet, thick honey inside the honeycomb. People who collect honey remove the combs. Last, the sweet honey is sold for us to eat.

9. **What is nectar?**
- Ⓐ a flower
- Ⓑ a watery substance that bees sip from flowers
- Ⓒ another name for honey
- Ⓓ a part of a bee's body that makes honey

10. **What would happen if the bees didn't have honey bags?**
- Ⓕ They couldn't make honey.
- Ⓖ They would fly in circles.
- Ⓗ They couldn't find flowers.
- Ⓙ They wouldn't be able to see.

11. **What happens after the bees put the nectar into their hives?**
- Ⓐ They fly from flower to flower.
- Ⓑ They collect the nectar.
- Ⓒ The bees sip the nectar from flowers.
- Ⓓ Most of the water leaves or evaporates.

12. **If you were a honey collector, where would you go to find honey?**
- Ⓕ in the store
- Ⓖ in the honeybees' hive
- Ⓗ in your house
- Ⓙ in the sand

READING PRACTICE TEST

● **Part 3: Story Comprehension (cont.)**

Directions: Read or listen to the paragraphs below that tell about a mom who lost her spaghetti. Then answer the questions.

The Investigation

The bowl sat empty. "Oh, no! My spaghetti is missing!" shrieked Mom. "I was supposed to take it to the school potluck tonight. What am I going to do?"

I decided to help my mom find her lost spaghetti. "Don't panic Mom, I'll look for clues," I said as I started looking around. The spaghetti had been in the bowl, on the counter, near the sink. First, I ran outside to check for footprints. There were none! It must have been an inside job.

Who would be my first suspect? I went to my baby sister Laurie's room. I checked in her crib, in her toy box, and in the closet. There was no sign of the spaghetti.

Next, I went to question my second suspect. I asked Dad if he had seen anything unusual. He had been mowing the lawn and didn't know anything about the case.

My leads seemed to be vanishing. Could a thief have come into our house and helped himself to dinner? Had aliens zapped it aboard their spaceship?

I looked around. Suddenly, I noticed through the open window two birds carrying long, red-and-white worms in their beaks. The Case of the Missing Spaghetti was closed!

13. What is the solution to The Case of the Missing Spaghetti?

- (A) Dad took the spaghetti.
- (B) Laurie ate the spaghetti.
- (C) Birds took the spaghetti.
- (D) Mom had put the spaghetti in the fridge.

14. Who was the second suspect?

- (F) baby Laurie
- (G) Mom
- (H) Dad
- (J) the birds

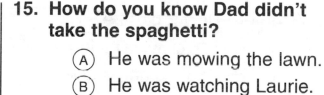

15. How do you know Dad didn't take the spaghetti?

- (A) He was mowing the lawn.
- (B) He was watching Laurie.
- (C) He liked pizza better.
- (D) Dad didn't like to investigate.

16. Why might the birds have taken the spaghetti?

- (F) They liked Italian food.
- (G) They thought they were worms.
- (H) They wanted to try something different.
- (J) They needed to make a nest.

GO ON

READING PRACTICE TEST

● **Part 3: Story Comprehension (cont.)**

Directions: Read or listen to the paragraphs below that tell about a boy who builds a robot. Then answer the questions.

Bert, the Inventor

Every day after school, Bert locked himself in his bedroom. He was working on a secret project. He didn't tell anyone what he was doing. Not even his best friend, Larry.

Bert finally finished. He had made a robot that looked exactly like himself. The robot had orange hair, freckles, and glasses. The robot and Bert both talked in a squeaky voice. "Life is going to be easy now!" exclaimed Bert. "I'm going to send my robot to school while I stay home and play."

The next morning the robot ate breakfast. Then he rode the bus to school. After school the bus dropped the robot back home. The robot knocked on the door.

"Sweetie, I am so glad you're home. I really missed you!" said Mom. Then, she took the robot into the kitchen and gave him a snack before dinner.

"We had lots of fun at school today," said the robot. "We went to the space museum. I got to try on a real space suit. It was too big for me but the teacher took my picture."

Bert was listening outside the kitchen. He was sad. He wanted to be an astronaut someday. He decided this wasn't a good idea. So the next day, Bert went to school himself.

17. What did Bert look like?

- (A) He had curly hair and was tall.
- (B) He had red hair and wore a cap.
- (C) He was short with blonde hair.
- (D) He had orange hair, freckles, and glasses.

18. Why did Bert decide to go to school himself?

- (F) He missed his mom's smile.
- (G) He missed going to the space museum.
- (H) He missed his friend Larry.
- (J) He missed eating breakfast and going to school.

19. Where does this story take place?

- (A) at school
- (B) at the grocery store
- (C) at Larry's house
- (D) at Bert's house

20. Why did Bert create the robot?

- (F) He wanted to make life easier and have the robot go to school for him.
- (G) His mom was feeling sick and needed help cleaning.
- (H) He didn't want to be friends with Larry anymore.
- (J) He was sad that he didn't have any brothers.

STOP

LANGUAGE: LISTENING

● **Lesson 1: Listening Skills**

Directions: Listen to the story. Then choose the best answer to each question.

Example

A. John was going on vacation with his family. They decided to go to Florida. Dad packed the car and John took his pillow. When they got there, they were going to stay with his grandparents. How was John traveling?

Ⓐ   Ⓑ   Ⓒ

**Clue** Remember, read or listen carefully to the story and look at all of the pictures.

● **Practice**

1. Before bed you can find Tony looking out his window. Tony loves to look through his telescope. His grandpa sometimes looks with him. He points out different things in the night sky. What does Tony see in the night sky?

Ⓐ   Ⓑ   Ⓒ

2. Lucy was getting ready to go to the grocery store with her mom. Lucy's mom never let her go anywhere in a car without buckling her seatbelt. She climbed into the car and started telling her mom what she wanted to buy at the store. Lucy's mom wouldn't start the car until Lucy did what?

Ⓕ   Ⓖ   Ⓗ

3. Pierce's dad is going on a business trip to Texas. He has to be at the airport very early in the morning. Pierce and his mom are going to take his dad out to breakfast. What will Pierce's dad ride in to get to Texas?

Ⓐ   Ⓑ   Ⓒ

LANGUAGE: LISTENING

● Lesson 2: Listening Skills

Directions: Read these words. Which one is different from the other three?

Example

A.
- (A) train
- (B) car
- (C) mule
- (D) plane

 Clue If you are not sure which answer is correct, take your best guess.

● Practice

1.
- (A) turtle
- (B) fish
- (C) shark
- (D) tiger

2.
- (F) teddy bear
- (G) doll
- (H) tree
- (J) toy car

3.
- (A) chair
- (B) desk
- (C) pencil
- (D) sink

4.
- (F) grass
- (G) dirt
- (H) carpet
- (J) flower

5.
- (A) fork
- (B) stove
- (C) spoon
- (D) knife

6.
- (F) happy
- (G) upset
- (H) angry
- (J) mad

STOP

LANGUAGE: LISTENING
SAMPLE TEST

● **Directions:** Listen to your teacher read the questions below. Then choose the best answer.

Examples

A. Yesterday Marty went to the dirt bike races. Marty loved to watch the riders jump in the air and speed through the sand. He had a great day with his dad. What does Marty look like?

 (A)   (B)   (C)

Read these words. Which one is different from the other three?

B.
- (F) hot dog
- (G) cake
- (H) cookies
- (J) ice cream

---

1. The Lee family likes that they have so many neighbors. They live on the third floor of their building. The Lee's children have many friends that they play with after school. Where does the Lee family live?

(A)   (B)   (C)

2. Abbey was traveling to see her aunt in New York. Her mom helped her get on the plane. Abbey was excited. She had a seat by the window. She thought she might get lonely because there was no one sitting next to her. Where is Abbey sitting?

(F)   (G)   (H)

3.
- (A) nose
- (B) head
- (C) toe
- (D) eye

4.
- (F) whiskers
- (G) finger
- (H) paws
- (J) tail

5.
- (A) book
- (B) chapter
- (C) page
- (D) computer

6.
- (F) shouting
- (G) picking
- (H) talking
- (J) whispering

STOP

1-57768-722-1 *Spectrum Test Practice 2*

Name _____ Date_____

LANGUAGE: MECHANICS

● **Lesson 3: Capitalization**

Directions: Which word in the sentence needs to be capitalized?

A. Football practice will start on monday.

    (A) Practice

    (B) Will

    (C) On

    (D) Monday

 Clue Sentences begin with capital letters. Important words in a sentence begin with capital letters.

● **Practice**

1. My friends will visit us on thanksgiving.

    (A) Friends

    (B) Visit

    (C) Us

    (D) Thanksgiving

2. Jake is going to the movies with his dad on saturday.

    (F) Going

    (G) Movies

    (H) Saturday

    (J) His

3. Donald and gordy like to visit Brook Manor.

    (A) Gordy

    (B) Like

    (C) To

    (D) Visit

4. Lily lived in Mexico but now she lives in america.

    (F) Lived

    (G) But

    (H) Lives

    (J) America

5. Marisa went to ohio to go shopping.

    (A) Went

    (B) To

    (C) Ohio

    (D) Shopping

6. her favorite animal to visit at the zoo is the kangaroo.

    (F) Her

    (G) Favorite

    (H) Animal

    (J) Zoo

STOP

Name _____ Date _____

LANGUAGE: MECHANICS

● **Lesson 4: Punctuation**

Directions: Read the sentences. Choose the correct punctuation mark that is needed.

Examples

A. **The phone is ringing**

   (A) .

   (B) !

   (C) ?

   (D) none

Donald takes Dudley to the store to buy a big bag of dog food. <u>Each dog food maker says that his dog food is the best</u>
                                  (B)

B.   (F) best?

     (G) best.

     (H) best!

 Clue Look for missing punctuation at the end of the sentence.

● **Practice**

1. **Watch out, the board is falling**

   (A) ?

   (B) .

   (C) !

   (D) none

2. **What do you think Mom will buy at the grocery store**

   (F) .

   (G) ?

   (H) !

   (J) none

3. **A family called the Magroons moved into the neighborhood**

   (A) !

   (B) ?

   (C) .

   (D) none

4. **Where is Nicky going with her ball**

   (F) ?

   (G) .

   (H) !

   (J) none

<u>The window was open in the kitchen</u>
                           (5)
When it started to rain, I ran to close it. I got there just in time. <u>Wow, it rained a lot</u>
                           (6)

5. (A) kitchen!

   (B) kitchen?

   (C) kitchen.

6. (F) lot?

   (G) lot!

   (H) lot.

STOP

Name _____ Date_____

LANGUAGE: MECHANICS

● **Lesson 5: Capitalization and Punctuation**

Directions: Read the sentences. Choose the best answer.

Examples

What sentence is capitalized and punctuated correctly?

A.
- Ⓐ My birthday is in october.
- Ⓑ last fall it was awfully warm?
- Ⓒ We plant our garden in June.

Look at the underlined part. Which corrections does it need?

B.

> **Monty Nelson**
> **368 King Street**
> <u>wilson pennsylvania 18302</u>

- Ⓕ wilson Pennsylvania 18302
- Ⓖ Wilson, pennsylvania 18302
- Ⓗ Wilson, Pennsylvania 18302

 Clue — Look for errors in capitalization. Then look for errors in punctuation.

● **Practice**

Choose the sentence with no errors.

1.
- Ⓐ Pass the ham to randy.
- Ⓑ Nothing is in the bag.
- Ⓒ dont' forget your coat

2.
- Ⓕ mark went to the mall
- Ⓖ I love to play soccer!
- Ⓗ why arent' you coming for dinner?

3.
- Ⓐ Stay right where you are bonnie!
- Ⓑ Go home right Now
- Ⓒ Will you please take me, Dad?

> _____ (4)
> _____ (5)
>   Thank you for the basketball.
> I have used it already.
>   _____ (6)

4.
- Ⓕ January 5, 2002
- Ⓖ january 5, 2002
- Ⓗ january 5 2002

5.
- Ⓐ dear dad
- Ⓑ Dear dad
- Ⓒ Dear Dad,

6.
- Ⓕ with love
- Ⓖ With love,
- Ⓗ with love,

GO ON

Published by Spectrum. Copyright protected.

1-57768-722-1 *Spectrum Test Practice 2*

Name _____ Date _____

LANGUAGE: MECHANICS

● **Lesson 5: Capitalization and Punctuation (cont.)**
  Directions: Read the story. Look at the underlined part. Choose the answer
  that shows the correct capitalization and punctuation.

Examples

On his way home from the <u>park</u>
                          (C)
<u>marcus</u> finds a baseball mitt under a

bush. Who could it belong <u>to marcus</u>
                           (D)
picked up the mitt and looked around

for its owner.

C.
  (A) park! Marcus
  (B) park, Marcus
  (C) park marcus.

D.
  (F) to? Marcus
  (G) to! Marcus
  (H) to, Marcus

One holiday is special to our family.

It is <u>Labor day</u> We volunteer at a local
        (7)
hospital so some of the workers can

take the day off. It <u>doesnt</u> bother us to
                      (8)
work on this holiday.

7.
  (A) labor day
  (B) Labor Day.
  (C) labor Day?

8.
  (F) doesn't
  (G) does'nt
  (H) doesn't'

Summer ends in a few weeks.

I made some nice friends. We even had

a special celebration for the <u>fourth of</u>
                                        (9)
<u>july</u> I loved all of the fireworks, and

<u>i cant</u> wait until next year's celebration!
 (10)

9.
  (A) Fourth of july!
  (B) fourth of july?
  (C) Fourth of July.

10.
  (F) I can't
  (G) i cant'
  (H) i ca'nt

STOP

63
1-57768-722-1 *Spectrum Test Practice 2*

Name _____   Date_____

● **Directions:** Which word in the sentence needs to be capitalized?

Example

A. **Monday, mandy has a band concert.**

   (A) Mandy

   (B) Has

   (C) Band

   (D) Concert

Sentences begin with capital letters. Important words in a sentence begin with capital letters.

1. **Joel is taking a trip to france in the fall.**

   (A) Taking

   (B) Trip

   (C) France

   (D) Fall

2. **My best friend, matt, lives in New York.**

   (F) Friend

   (G) Matt

   (H) Lives

   (J) In

3. **I went to east Oakview Elementary when I was in second grade.**

   (A) East

   (B) When

   (C) Second

   (D) Grade

4. **Grandma and Grandpa fly in from florida.**

   (F) Fly

   (G) In

   (H) And

   (J) Florida

5. **My aunt Marta will be coming to my dance recital.**

   (A) Will

   (B) Aunt

   (C) Dance

   (D) Recital

6. **The kids that belong to the Sunshine club will sell cookies tomorrow.**

   (F) Kids

   (G) Club

   (H) Cookie

   (J) Tomorrow

GO ON

Name _____ Date_____

● **Directions:** Read the sentences. Choose the correct punctuation mark that is needed. If no punctuation is needed, choose none.

Examples

B.   **The boy ran out the door**

  Ⓕ .

  Ⓖ !

  Ⓗ ?

  Ⓙ none

Mom and Dad bought six extra tickets for the play. She was excited for everyone to come see the play. Maria will play the old <u>woman</u>

(C)

C.   Ⓐ woman?

  Ⓑ woman.

  Ⓒ woman!

Look for missing punctuation at the end of the sentence.

7.   **Did Leo and Elaine finish the project**

  Ⓐ ?

  Ⓑ .

  Ⓒ !

  Ⓓ none

8.   **The book she read to the class was very funny**

  Ⓕ .

  Ⓖ ?

  Ⓗ !

  Ⓙ none

9.   **Hey, wait until there are no cars before you cross the street**

  Ⓐ !

  Ⓑ ?

  Ⓒ .

  Ⓓ none

10. **Why isn't Sarah happy today**

  Ⓕ ?

  Ⓖ .

  Ⓗ !

  Ⓙ none

While Mom and Dad were cooking dinner, Jared came in the <u>kitchen what</u>

(11)

<u>are</u> you <u>making I</u> am so hungry," Jared

(12)

asked his parents. Mom smiled at Jared.

They were cooking his favorite meal.

11.   Ⓐ kitchen. What are

  Ⓑ kitchen? What are

  Ⓒ kitchen. "What are

12.   Ⓕ making? I

  Ⓖ making. I

  Ⓗ making! I

GO ON

Name _____ Date _____

● **Directions:** Read the sentences. Choose the best answer.

Examples

What sentence is capitalized and punctuated correctly?

D.
- Ⓕ Valentine's Day is in february
- Ⓖ Where does sylvia work?
- Ⓗ In January, my brother and I have snowball fights.

Look at the underlined part. Which corrections does it need?

E.

> **Brian Phebus**
> **2629 Foster Ave.**
> **<u>newago michigan 85623</u>**

- Ⓐ newago, Michigan 85623
- Ⓑ Newago, Michigan 85623
- Ⓒ Newago, michigan 85623

Choose the sentence with no errors.

13.
- Ⓐ Please kalid, will you fix my computer.
- Ⓑ I think halloween is a fun holiday.
- Ⓒ Be sure to be at school on time!

14.
- Ⓕ Michael went camping in the Hidden Woods.
- Ⓖ I love to eat ice cream
- Ⓗ why is grandma mowing the lawn today?

15.
- Ⓐ sara and marilyn went to the sahara desert.
- Ⓑ get out of my way!
- Ⓒ Please help Dad take the trash outside.

> _____ (16)
> _____ (17)
>   Please come to my house for a birthday party. Jacob will be 9 years old! The party will be at our house on Thursday, July 24. Hope you can come!
>   _____ (18)

16.
- Ⓕ july 16 2002
- Ⓖ July 16, 2002
- Ⓗ July 16 2002

17.
- Ⓐ dear Erik
- Ⓑ Dear erik,
- Ⓒ Dear Erik,

18.
- Ⓕ Yours truly,
- Ⓖ Yours truly
- Ⓗ yours truly

GO ON

LANGUAGE: MECHANICS
SAMPLE TEST (cont.)

● **Directions:** Read the story. Look at the underlined part. Choose the answer that shows the correct capitalization and punctuation.

Examples

Simon's <u>cat pinkie</u> had 5 kittens. He
     (F)
was hoping that he could find good

homes for them. He made a sign that

said, "Who would like <u>a kitten</u>
           (G)

F.
- (F) cat! Pinkie
- (G) cat, Pinkie,
- (H) Cat Pinkie!

G.
- (A) a kitten"
- (B) a Kitten?"
- (C) a kitten?"

We decided to spend our vacation at

the <u>grand canyon</u> We were going to
    (19)
camp there for a week. If it <u>isnt</u> too
           (20)
much money, we even want to take a

ride to the bottom of the canyon.

19.
- (A) Grand Canyon.
- (B) grand Canyon.
- (C) Grand Canyon?

20.
- (F) isnt'
- (G) is'nt
- (H) isn't

<u>mr james</u> teaches at <u>West orchard</u>
 (21)   **(22)**
school. He loves teaching about Native

Americans.

21.
- (A) Mr. James
- (B) mr! James
- (C) Mr. james

22.
- (F) west orchard school. He
- (G) West Orchard School. He
- (H) west orchard school. he

STOP

LANGUAGE: EXPRESSION

● **Lesson 6: Usage**

Directions: Look at the sentence. What word or phrase should go in the blank or should be substituted for the underlined part?

Examples

A. He makes friends _____ than his brother.

    Ⓐ easy

    Ⓑ easiest

    Ⓒ easily

    Ⓓ easier

B. <u>Suki</u> was more frightened than Jawan.

    Ⓕ Its

    Ⓖ She

    Ⓗ Her

    Ⓙ Them

Clue Stay with your first answer. It is usually right.

● **Practice**

1. Leah is the _____ at math.

    Ⓐ better

    Ⓑ good

    Ⓒ best

    Ⓓ well

2. Aunt Jeanne is the _____ teacher I know.

    Ⓕ finest

    Ⓖ fine

    Ⓗ finer

    Ⓙ finally

3. Hunter likes to draw _____ than his sister does.

    Ⓐ most

    Ⓑ best

    Ⓒ bestest

    Ⓓ more

4. The movie that <u>Sam and Amy</u> watched was very funny.

    Ⓕ he

    Ⓖ they

    Ⓗ them

    Ⓙ us

5. We found <u>the shoe</u> in the bottom of the box.

    Ⓐ me

    Ⓑ there

    Ⓒ she

    Ⓓ it

6. Please help <u>your brother</u> clean his room.

    Ⓕ her

    Ⓖ we

    Ⓗ him

    Ⓙ it

STOP

LANGUAGE: EXPRESSION

● Lesson 7: Usage

Directions: Read the sentences. Which part of the sentences is not correct? Example A has been done for you.

Examples

A.
(A) The little baby spider climbed
(B) up to the top of the leaf.
(●) Then we lets out a long strand of silk.

Practice on this one.

B.
(F) The wind turned the
(G) silk into shes balloon
(H) and lifted the spider away.

● Practice

Clue Stay with your first answer. It is usually right.

1. (A) I have a new puppy.
(B) Her name is Lady.
(C) Lady was the prettier dog at the pet store.

2. (F) Lady is small now.
(G) But, she will not never grow to be the biggest dog.
(H) I think she is the smartest.

3. (A) Lady loves to play with my brother and me.
(B) Us love when she plays fetch.
(C) Her favorite game is tug of war.

4. (F) Jan live in the country.
(G) She asked for a pony.
(H) Her parents said she must learn how to care for a pony.

5. (A) Jan got books about ponies.
(B) She talked to friends who had ponies.
(C) She her listed three rules about caring for a pony.

6. (F) A pony need a clean, dry stalls.
(G) It needs a large area outside to get exercise.
(H) A pony eats grain and hay twice a day.

STOP

Name _____   Date_____

LANGUAGE: EXPRESSION

● **Lesson 8: Sentences**

Directions: Read the sentence. What phrase fits in the blank?

Example

A. The _____ has lots of apples.

(A) green lawn in the back

(B) big tree next to the house

(C) over the house

(D) tree around the

 Clue If you are not sure which answer is correct, take your best guess. Eliminate answer choices you know are wrong.

● **Practice**

1. You need a ticket _____.

   (A) to fly in a plane

   (B) to bake

   (C) to drive in the

   (D) in the row

2. _____ took place last Saturday.

   (F) Dogs and cats

   (G) Sunny day

   (H) The picnic

   (J) Running feet

3. Alexis and her cat, Boots, like to run and _____.

   (A) around the bush

   (B) leaving on the hat

   (C) with the other children

   (D) play at the park

4. Tony is the boy who _____.

   (F) eating the cookies

   (G) takes his time doing homework

   (H) until he stops running

   (J) needing to go to sleep

5. I put _____ and went for a ride.

   (A) answer my mom

   (B) around the corner

   (C) on my bike helmet

   (D) for my birthday gift

6. Dan walked _____ each day.

   (F) along five miles to

   (G) leaving his jacket

   (H) so mom would

   (J) five miles to school

GO ON

LANGUAGE: EXPRESSION

● **Lesson 8: Sentences (cont.)**

Directions: Read the sentence. Which one is a complete sentence?

Example

B. (F) This is my book.

(G) These there clocks set wrong.

(H) Who going to the wedding?

(J) Where she gone?

 Clue   A correct sentence contains a subject and a verb. It expresses a complete idea.

● **Practice**

7. (A) On the light.
   (B) Went down the hill.
   (C) She ate the candy.
   (D) Pink and blue ribbons.

8. (F) Picked from the tree.
   (G) Seeing the boy and girl.
   (H) The picnic.
   (J) Natalie rolled in the sand.

9. (A) Minka sat in the sun.
   (B) She to go school.
   (C) Dad cookies and cakes to eat.
   (D) Miss Read likes when her students.

10. (F) My wagon in the garage.
    (G) Your brother went with you.
    (H) Juliet saw what she knew was.
    (J) Mary Ella and felt like she had a fever.

11. (A) The family had fun at the circus.
    (B) The children cried and wanted lots of.
    (C) She the keys to the car.
    (D) Arleen bike color blue.

12. (F) Feet, toes, and knees.
    (G) How she like to?
    (H) The red balloon was still in her hand.
    (J) Won the prize last night at the birthday party.

Name _____ Date _____

LANGUAGE: EXPRESSION

● **Lesson 9: Paragraphs**

Directions: Read the paragraph. Which choice best fits in the blank?

Example

A. **Makayla and Elisabeth were hot. _____ Then they built a sand castle.**

   (A) They played in the snow.

   (B) The ocean is a fun place to play.

   (C) They played in the ocean water.

   (D) Sharks and dolphins live in the ocean.

● **Practice**  **A paragraph should focus on one idea. All the sentences in a paragraph should be related.**

1. **_____ He raked them into a pile. Later his dad would help him with the backyard.**

   (A) Leaves are different colors in the fall.

   (B) Austin walked through the red and yellow leaves.

   (C) Trees are beautiful when they change color.

   (D) The bird lived in the oak tree.

2. **Cedrick and his grandpa worked in the garden. They planted corn, beans, and lettuce. _____**

   (F) Dogs and cats like gardens.

   (G) Sunny days are great for eating ice cream.

   (H) The picnic was fun.

   (J) They were excited to plant lots of good vegetables to eat.

3. **My mom is the lady _____.**

   (A) eats lots of food

   (B) loves her children

   (C) dances with my dad

   (D) standing by the red car

4. **I went swimming _____ on Sunday. My cousins were there too. After we swam, we went on a boat ride. We had a great day.**

   (F) at the lake

   (G) around the next street

   (H) on the swing set

   (J) near the garage

5. **He was very upset yesterday. He didn't sleep well the night before. He really needed _____.**

   (A) dancing to the music

   (B) sleeping for five hours

   (C) that weren't scary

   (D) to take a long nap

GO ON

1-57768-722-1 *Spectrum Test Practice 2*

Name _____   Date_____

LANGUAGE: EXPRESSION

● **Lesson 9: Paragraphs (cont.)**
Directions: Read the paragraph. Answer the questions that follow.

Example

Grandmother and Kyler put on coats, hats, gloves, and boots. They went outside to make a snowman. Grandmother started rolling the head while Kyler looked for sticks to make the arms.

B. **Which sentence does not belong?**

F Their favorite pastime was reading stories at night.

G Kyler had buttons in her pocket to make the eyes.

H They knew to dress warm.

 **Clue** A paragraph should focus on one idea. All the sentences in a paragraph should be related.

● **Practice**

Lions and house cats belong in the cat family. Lions are big animals. They roar loudly. Cats are small animals. They meow softly. Lions and cats both have fur. They have sharp claws and are good hunters. Lions live in zoos and jungles. House cats live with families.

6. **Which sentence does not belong in this paragraph?**

F Lions and cats both have whiskers.

G Cheetahs can run very fast.

H Baby lions are called cubs, and baby cats are called kittens.

7. **Which sentence does belong in this paragraph?**

A House cats sometimes purr when you pet them.

B Zebras live in Africa.

C Jaguars are good hunters.

8. **Nico needs to write a second paragraph. His paragraph will be about another type of animal that belongs in the cat family. What should he do before he writes his paragraph?**

F Think about what house cats and lions might do to a cheetah.

G Write a letter to his uncle asking for information about his house cat.

H Write down what he knows about the cat family.

9. **What should the topic of Nico's second paragraph be?**

A what kittens look like when they are young

B cheetahs and how they are a part of the cat family

C how cats can be trained to play fetch

LANGUAGE: EXPRESSION
SAMPLE TEST

● **Directions:** Read the sentences. Choose the correct answer.

Examples

A. Brad and Jeff_____.

- (A) laughing in the back of the car.
- (B) worked in the garden.
- (C) in the road playing street hockey.
- (D) eats lots of vegetables.

Carefully read the choices. Which one is written correctly?

B.
- (F) Tim clean his room.
- (G) The boys watcheded the hippo take a bath.
- (H) Ben likes to ride ponies.
- (J) The man in the black suit is the most richest.

If you are not sure which answer is correct, take your best guess. Eliminate answer choices you know are wrong.

1. _____a big sand castle at the beach.
- (A) Alicia in the blue swim suit
- (B) birds over the water
- (C) Alicia made
- (D) Jake went

2. **How many _____ can I take in my lunch?**
- (F) cookie
- (G) picnic
- (H) piece
- (J) cookies

3. **Kim helped _____.**
- (A) around the house.
- (B) want lots of sunny days.
- (C) with many friends.
- (D) played basketball.

4.
- (F) You need a ticket to flies in a plane.
- (G) Some people for a laugh.
- (H) Wearing a seat belt.
- (J) This is my seat.

5.
- (A) The watch in my pocket.
- (B) He wore his bestest clothes for the first day of school.
- (C) She planned to go on a boat ride with Uncle Michael.
- (D) Where she going?

6.
- (F) Like my shoes?
- (G) Please, buy some milk.
- (H) She see her cat on the roof.
- (J) Omar dog lick his neck.

GO ON

Name _____ Date _____

● **Directions:** Read the paragraph. Which choice best fits in the blank?

Example

C. **Tyler sits at his desk reading. _____ They are studying weather for the whole month of May.**

- Ⓐ May is a good month to plant flowers.
- Ⓑ He is very interested in rain.
- Ⓒ His book is all about weather.
- Ⓓ Tyler's desk is very messy.

A paragraph should focus on one idea. All the sentences in a paragraph should be related.

7. **_____ She takes her sled outside. Missy slides down the hill.**
- Ⓐ Who loves the snow?
- Ⓑ Snowmen are fun to build.
- Ⓒ A sled costs ten dollars.
- Ⓓ Missy puts on her coat, mittens, and hat.

8. **The family was going camping. Mom packed the food. _____ Cory packed the sleeping bags.**
- Ⓕ Dad packed the tent.
- Ⓖ They went to a movie.
- Ⓗ Cory always waits his turn.
- Ⓙ Mom calls Grandma.

9. **_____ It has four legs and a tail. It hides inside its shell when it gets scared.**
- Ⓐ Some cats like to drink milk.
- Ⓑ Robins lay blue eggs.
- Ⓒ My brother wants a fish tank.
- Ⓓ A turtle lives in water and on land.

10. **Jenny helps her Mother. _____ She sets the table. Jenny cleans her room. They work together.**
- Ⓕ She didn't like her brother.
- Ⓖ She folds clothes.
- Ⓗ She went to sleep.
- Ⓙ She rode her bike.

11. **My brother went _____ to the doctor. He had to sit in the waiting room for a long time.**
- Ⓐ to my mom
- Ⓑ around the house
- Ⓒ sitting on the chair
- Ⓓ with my sister

12. **Selena asked _____ the math problem. Selena was confused.**
- Ⓕ under the desk was the paper
- Ⓖ her teacher to explain
- Ⓗ until we had milk for lunch
- Ⓙ around the school

GO ON

Name_____ Date_____

● **Directions:** Read the paragraph. Answer the questions that follow.

Example

> Ben and Troy visited the city zoo. The bears and lions were asleep. Troy fed peanuts to an elephant. Ben rode a pony.
>
> **D. Which sentence does belong in the paragraph?**
>
>   Ⓕ Ben rode a fast ride at the amusement park.
>
>   Ⓖ Ben and Troy had a great day at the zoo.
>
>   Ⓗ Ben and Troy went to the baseball game.

A paragraph should focus on one idea. All the sentences in a paragraph should be related.

> Dear Aunt Elida,
>
> You will never believe what happened yesterday! I was walking down the street when a fire truck went by me. I followed the truck. It went to my best friend Coby's house. Coby was outside with his family. Their house had caught on fire. Because they had practiced fire drills, they made it out safely. The firefighters put out the fire. The kitchen was the only room damaged. Coby and his family are doing fine.
>
> Love, Chantal

13. Which sentence does not belong in this paragraph?

Ⓐ I went to get ice cream.

Ⓑ Coby was upset about the fire.

Ⓒ Coby's mom and dad said everything would be fine.

14. Which sentence does belong in this paragraph?

Ⓕ Firefighters wear helmets.

Ⓖ The firefighters that helped Coby's family were great.

Ⓗ Coby's family is going on a trip to Colorado.

15. If Chantal wants to tell her aunt about practicing fire safety, what should the topic of Chantal's second paragraph be?

Ⓐ how she misses her aunt

Ⓑ going to Suzie's house

Ⓒ how to practice fire safety

16. Which sentence would not belong in this second paragraph?

Ⓕ Never leave matches around the house.

Ⓖ If your clothes catch on fire, stop, drop, and roll.

Ⓗ Coby's family had friends.

1-57768-722-1 *Spectrum Test Practice 2*

LANGUAGE: SPELLING

● **Lesson 10: Spelling Skills**

Directions: Read the sentences. Which word fits in the sentence and is spelled correctly?

Example

A. Did you _____who was there?

- (A) notise
- (B) notice
- (C) notisce
- (D) nootis

Clue If an item is too difficult, skip it and move on to another one. Come back later to the item you skipped.

● **Practice**

1. The lake is _____ that hill.
   - (A) beayond
   - (B) beyon
   - (C) beyond
   - (D) beyont

2. Be _____ near the pond.
   - (F) carefull
   - (G) cairful
   - (H) carful
   - (J) careful

3. She went to the pool _____ she wanted to swim.
   - (A) becuz
   - (B) because
   - (C) beecus
   - (D) becuas

4. Do you _____ which way the twins went?
   - (F) kno
   - (G) noow
   - (H) kow
   - (J) know

5. She was sure the teacher would stop the _____.
   - (A) fight
   - (B) fiet
   - (C) figt
   - (D) fieat

6. The spinner _____ stopped on the red space.
   - (F) fineally
   - (G) finally
   - (H) fineulee
   - (J) finelly

STOP

LANGUAGE: SPELLING

● **Lesson 11: Spelling Skills**

Directions: Carefully read the words. Choose the word that is <u>not</u> spelled correctly.

Example

A.
- Ⓐ chaire
- Ⓑ tree
- Ⓒ subtract
- Ⓓ around

 Clue Read all the answer choices before choosing the one you think is correct.

● **Practice**

1.
- Ⓐ hidden
- Ⓑ never
- Ⓒ windey
- Ⓓ plain

2.
- Ⓕ tiger
- Ⓖ sandwhich
- Ⓗ yellow
- Ⓙ bird

3.
- Ⓐ does
- Ⓑ didn't
- Ⓒ away
- Ⓓ befor

4.
- Ⓕ enuf
- Ⓖ high
- Ⓗ however
- Ⓙ idea

5.
- Ⓐ sleep
- Ⓑ shuld
- Ⓒ over
- Ⓓ maybe

6.
- Ⓕ right
- Ⓖ same
- Ⓗ papr
- Ⓙ teach

STOP

Name _____ Date_____

LANGUAGE: SPELLING

● **Lesson 12: Spelling Skills**

   Directions: Read the sentences. Look at the underlined words. Which one is not spelled <u>correctly</u>?

Example

A. Our <u>dailly</u> run is <u>about</u> two miles.
   (A)   (B)   (C)

 Clue If you are not sure which answer is correct, take your best guess. Eliminate answer choices you know are wrong.

● **Practice**

1. We <u>usuelly</u> arrive <u>around</u> <u>three</u> o'clock.
       (A)   (B)   (C)

2. <u>Did</u> you <u>forgit</u> <u>your</u> hat?
    (F)   (G)   (H)

3. Dad <u>rowsted</u> <u>some</u> corn for <u>dinner</u>.
        (A)   (B)   (C)

4. Call Mom <u>aftr</u> you get <u>home</u> <u>tomorrow</u>.
            (F)   (G)   (H)

5. Do you like to <u>build</u> sand <u>castles</u> when you are at the <u>beech</u>?
                   (A)   (B)   (C)

6. Jake's bus was ten <u>minutes</u> <u>laat</u> <u>today</u>.
                       (F)   (G)   (H)

LANGUAGE: SPELLING
SAMPLE TEST

● **Directions:** Read the sentences. Which word fits in the sentence and is spelled <u>correctly</u>?

Example

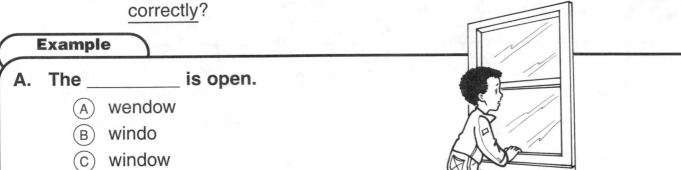

A. The _____ is open.

    Ⓐ wendow

    Ⓑ windo

    Ⓒ window

    Ⓓ windowe

**If an item is too difficult, skip it and move on to another one.
Come back later to the item you skipped.**

1. **Alan felt _____ in his new school.**

    Ⓐ loneley

    Ⓑ loanly

    Ⓒ loanley

    Ⓓ lonely

2. **A _____ blocked the sun.**

    Ⓕ clowd

    Ⓖ cloud

    Ⓗ clawd

    Ⓙ claud

3. **When did you _____ that bike?**

    Ⓐ buy

    Ⓑ bi

    Ⓒ bei

    Ⓓ bui

4. **I think blue is a _____ color than red.**

    Ⓕ bettr

    Ⓖ beter

    Ⓗ better

    Ⓙ betr

5. **On the map the state of Florida is _____ Georgia.**

    Ⓐ below

    Ⓑ beelow

    Ⓒ belo

    Ⓓ beloo

6. **My _____ has three cats and a dog.**

    Ⓕ teecher

    Ⓖ teachr

    Ⓗ teacher

    Ⓙ teechr

GO ON

LANGUAGE: SPELLING
SAMPLE TEST (cont.)

● **Directions:** Carefully read the words. Choose the word that is <u>not</u> spelled correctly.

Example

B.
(F) figt
(G) country
(H) done
(J) can't

Read all the answer choices before choosing the one you think is correct.

7.
(A) year
(B) yard
(C) way
(D) truble

10.
(F) next
(G) amung
(H) body
(J) have

8.
(F) anumal
(G) behind
(H) brought
(J) bike

11.
(A) green
(B) inside
(C) triing
(D) into

9.
(A) there
(B) time
(C) thees
(D) nice

12.
(F) just
(G) wrld
(H) being
(J) often

GO ON

LANGUAGE: SPELLING
SAMPLE TEST (cont.)

● **Directions:** Read the sentences. Look at the underlined words. Which one is not spelled correctly?

> **Example**
>
> C.   Jack <u>knew</u> there was going to be <u>trulbe</u> when the bats flew out of the <u>cave</u>.
>   Ⓐ   Ⓑ   Ⓒ

If you are not sure which answer is correct, take your best guess. Eliminate answer choices you know are wrong.

13. Are you <u>haveing</u> a <u>problem</u> <u>doing</u> your math?
     Ⓐ   Ⓑ   Ⓒ

14. She <u>kicked</u> the ball and it <u>went</u> <u>beetwen</u> the two players.
     Ⓕ   Ⓖ   Ⓗ

15. Mom <u>made</u> us <u>ware</u> our coats <u>outside</u>.
     Ⓐ   Ⓑ   Ⓒ

16. I <u>helped</u> my friend's <u>family</u> <u>paent</u> their fence.
     Ⓕ   Ⓖ   Ⓗ

17. You will be in the <u>first</u> <u>groop</u> to eat <u>lunch</u>.
     Ⓐ   Ⓑ   Ⓒ

18. Can you <u>beleeve</u> <u>they</u> are <u>going</u> to Hawaii?
     Ⓕ   Ⓖ   Ⓗ

STOP

Name _____ Date_____

LANGUAGE: STUDY SKILLS

● **Lesson 13: Study Skills**

Directions: Read the table of contents and index. Answer the questions that follow.

Examples

The following pages are from a book about art.

Table of Contents	
Painting 3	
Drawing.........................14	
Index 53	
Glossary 57	

Index	
colors 8, 22, 31	
museums 2,10,19, 35	
pencil 16	
water color paints 5	

A. What is the glossary used for?

- Ⓐ to find out about pencils
- Ⓑ to read about other kinds of art
- Ⓒ to look up key words you don't understand
- Ⓓ to find out if painting is fun

B. What pages would you look on to find out about museums?

- Ⓕ pages 8, 22, 31
- Ⓖ pages 2,10,19, 35
- Ⓗ page 14
- Ⓙ page 29

Clue Think about the question and look at all the choices before you choose an answer. The following are pages taken from a book about the different states in the U.S.A.

● **Practice**

Table of Contents	
Introduction 1	
Alabama....................................2	
Alaska 12	
Arizona....................................25	
Index 36	
Glossary..................................49	

Index	
Atlanta, Georgia.......................34	
education 7,15,19, 27	
industry 5, 23	
population 4,17, 26, 32	
resources 6,13, 25	
trivia 11, 29, 46	

1. If you were doing a report on Alaska, what pages would you turn to?

- Ⓐ pages 12–24
- Ⓑ pages 34–45
- Ⓒ pages 46–54
- Ⓓ pages 2–11

2. Where should you look to find out about schools?

- Ⓕ under Georgia on page 34
- Ⓖ in the resource section
- Ⓗ in the education section
- Ⓙ under population on page 32

GO ON

1-57768-722-1 *Spectrum Test Practice 2*

Name _____   Date_____

● **Lesson 13: Study Skills (cont.)**

Directions: Read the questions carefully. Choose the correct answers.

> **Example**
>
> **C. Which words are in alphabetical order?**
>
> (A) cat, dog, light, star
>
> (B) dog, cat, light, star
>
> (C) star, light, cat, dog
>
> (D) light, cat, star, dog

 Remember when alphabetizing, if the first letters are the same, look at the next letter.

● **Practice**

3. **If the guide words at the top of your dictionary page are face—fish, which word will you find on the page?**

   (A) full

   (B) time

   (C) enough

   (D) factory

4. **Lucy is going to the store. She needs: milk, cat food, butter, eggs, ham, hot dogs, and soup. Put the list in alphabetical order. Which word comes after hot dogs?**

   (F) eggs

   (G) cat food

   (H) ham

   (J) milk

5. **Which set is in alphabetical order?**

   (A) bike, bus, came, done

   (B) bus, bike, done, came

   (C) came, done, bus, bike

   (D) bike, came, bus, done

6. **Which guide words should you look for if you are looking for the word mountain?**

   (F) math—mask

   (G) mother—mouth

   (H) math—meat

   (J) mystery—myth

7. **Which set is not in alphabetical order?**

   (A) day, deep, does

   (B) keep, just, line

   (C) heavy, help, inside

   (D) reason, sick, today

8. **Jason's birthday list has on it: a bike, board games, pants, a puppy, a snake, a football, and a soccer ball. Put the list in alphabetical order. Which word comes before pants?**

   (F) soccer ball

   (G) puppy

   (H) snake

   (J) football

GO ON

Name _____   Date _____

● **Lesson 13: Study Skills (cont.)**

Directions: Read the map. Choose the best answer to each question.

Example

D. **The route that bus 4 drives goes in which direction?**

   (F) west
   (G) east
   (H) south
   (J) north

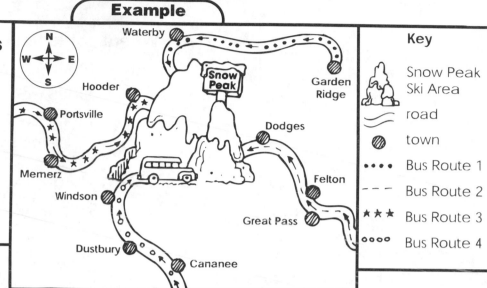

Key

Snow Peak Ski Area

~ road

◉ town

•••• Bus Route 1

- - - Bus Route 2

★★★ Bus Route 3

∘∘∘∘ Bus Route 4

● **Practice**   **Clue** Eliminate answer choices you know are wrong.

9. **Bus 4 picks up people from which towns?**

   (A) Windson, Dustbury, Cananee
   (B) Garden Ridge, Waterby
   (C) Great Pass, Felton, Dodges
   (D) Memerz, Portsville, Hooder

10. **Mitzi lives in Great Pass. Which bus will she ride?**

   (F) Bus 1
   (G) Bus 2
   (H) Bus 3
   (J) Bus 4

11. **In which direction does the route for Bus 2 go?**

   (A) southeast
   (B) southwest
   (C) northwest
   (D) northeast

12. **Greg lives in Portsville. Which bus will he ride?**

   (F) Bus 1
   (G) Bus 2
   (H) Bus 3
   (J) Bus 4

13. **Bailey lives in Garden Ridge. Which bus will she ride?**

   (A) Bus 1
   (B) Bus 2
   (C) Bus 3
   (D) Bus 4

14. **Bus 1 picks up people from which towns?**

   (F) Windson, Dustbury, Cananee
   (G) Garden Ridge, Waterby
   (H) Great Pass, Felton, Dodges
   (J) Memerz, Portsville, Hooder

Name _____   Date_____

LANGUAGE: STUDY SKILLS
SAMPLE TEST

● **Directions:** Read the questions. Choose the correct answer.

Examples

Table of Contents

Use the table of contents above to answer questions 1–3.

A. **Where could you read about butterflies?**
- Ⓐ pages 2–15
- Ⓑ pages 16–24
- Ⓒ pages 25–38
- Ⓓ pages 39–52

B. **Which words are in alphabetical order?**
- Ⓕ bench, bridge, duck, swing, path
- Ⓖ bridge, bench, duck, swing, path
- Ⓗ duck, bench, bridge, path, swing
- Ⓙ bench, bridge, duck, path, swing

1. **Where can you find the meaning of a word?**
- Ⓐ pages 12–24
- Ⓑ index
- Ⓒ introduction
- Ⓓ glossary

2. **Where can Max find out which page is about spider webs?**
- Ⓕ under Ants on page 39
- Ⓖ in the glossary
- Ⓗ in the index
- Ⓙ in the introduction

3. **Where can Sue find information about bees?**
- Ⓐ pages 2–15
- Ⓑ pages 16–24
- Ⓒ pages 25–38
- Ⓓ pages 39–52

4. **Which set is in alphabetical order?**
- Ⓕ bakery, art, pet, bookstore
- Ⓖ art, bakery, bookstore, pet
- Ⓗ art, bookstore, bakery, pet
- Ⓙ art, pet, bakery, bookstore

5. **If the guide words are good— green, which word could you find on the dictionary page?**
- Ⓐ girl
- Ⓑ game
- Ⓒ had
- Ⓓ great

6. **Hannah wants to invite: Mark, Isabella, Nathan, and Makayla. After she puts her list in alphabetical order, who will be before Makayla?**
- Ⓕ Isabella
- Ⓖ Mark
- Ⓗ Nathan
- Ⓙ Makayla

GO ON

● **Directions:** Read the map. Choose the best answer to each question.

Example

C. About how many miles are there between Bright Pass and Summit Mountain?

(A) 50
(B) 15
(C) 5
(D) 2

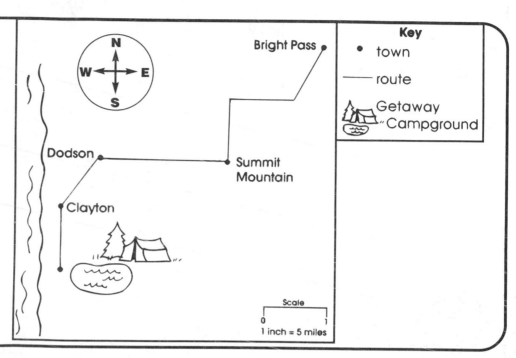

If you are not sure which answer is correct, take your best guess.
Eliminate answer choices you know are wrong.

7. **In which direction would you go if you were going from Dodson to Summit Mountain?**

(A) north
(B) south
(C) east
(D) west

8. **Sharon lives in Clayton and wants to go to Getaway Campground. How many miles will she travel?**

(F) 5
(G) 15
(H) 25
(J) 50

9. **Sam lives in Bright Pass and is going to Summit Mountain. In which direction must he travel first to get there?**

(A) southeast
(B) southwest
(C) northwest
(D) northeast

10. **Marie lives in Clayton and wants to go to Dodson. Which direction must she travel?**

(F) northeast
(G) northwest
(H) southeast
(J) southwest

 STOP

ANSWER SHEET

STUDENT'S NAME

LAST	FIRST	MI

(Bubble grid A–Z for each name column)

SCHOOL

TEACHER

FEMALE ○   MALE ○

BIRTH DATE

MONTH	DAY	YEAR
JAN ○	0 0	0
FEB ○	1 1	1
MAR ○	2 2	2
APR ○	3 3	3
MAY ○	4	4
JUN ○	5	5 5
JUL ○	6	6 6
AUG ○	7	7 7
SEP ○	8	8 8
OCT ○	9	9 9
NOV ○	0	
DEC ○		

GRADE
① ② ③

Part 1: LISTENING

A (A)(B)(C)   3 (A)(B)(C)(D)
B (F)(G)(H)(J)   4 (F)(G)(H)(J)
1 (A)(B)(C)   5 (A)(B)(C)(D)
2 (F)(G)(H)

Part 2: LANGUAGE MECHANICS

A (A)(B)(C)   3 (A)(B)(C)   C (A)(B)(C)   9 (A)(B)(C)
B (F)(G)(H)   4 (F)(G)(H)   D (F)(G)(H)   10 (F)(G)(H)
1 (A)(B)(C)   5 (A)(B)(C)   7 (A)(B)(C)
2 (F)(G)(H)   6 (F)(G)(H)   8 (F)(G)(H)

Part 3: LANGUAGE EXPRESSION

A (A)(B)(C)(D)   C (A)(B)(C)   13 (A)(B)(C)(D)   20 (F)(G)(H)(J)   27 (A)(B)(C)(D)   34 (F)(G)(H)
B (F)(G)(H)(J)   7 (A)(B)(C)   14 (F)(G)(H)(J)   21 (A)(B)(C)(D)   28 (F)(G)(H)(J)   35 (A)(B)(C)
1 (A)(B)(C)(D)   8 (F)(G)(H)   15 (A)(B)(C)(D)   22 (F)(G)(H)(J)   29 (A)(B)(C)(D)   36 (F)(G)(H)
2 (F)(G)(H)(J)   9 (A)(B)(C)   16 (F)(G)(H)(J)   23 (A)(B)(C)(D)   30 (F)(G)(H)(J)   37 (A)(B)(C)
3 (A)(B)(C)(D)   10 (F)(G)(H)   17 (A)(B)(C)(D)   24 (F)(G)(H)(J)   G (A)(B)(C)   38 (F)(G)(H)
4 (F)(G)(H)(J)   11 (A)(B)(C)   18 (F)(G)(H)(J)   F (F)(G)(H)(J)   31 (A)(B)(C)   39 (A)(B)(C)(D)
5 (A)(B)(C)(D)   12 (F)(G)(H)   E (A)(B)(C)(D)   25 (A)(B)(C)(D)   32 (F)(G)(H)
6 (F)(G)(H)(J)   D (F)(G)(H)(J)   19 (A)(B)(C)(D)   26 (F)(G)(H)(J)   33 (A)(B)(C)

Part 4: SPELLING

A (A)(B)(C)(D)   5 (A)(B)(C)(D)   8 (F)(G)(H)(J)
1 (A)(B)(C)(D)   6 (F)(G)(H)(J)   9 (A)(B)(C)(D)
2 (F)(G)(H)(J)   B (F)(G)(H)(J)   10 (F)(G)(H)
3 (A)(B)(C)(D)   C (A)(B)(C)   11 (A)(B)(C)
4 (F)(G)(H)(J)   7 (A)(B)(C)(D)   12 (F)(G)(H)

Part 5: STUDY SKILLS

A (A)(B)(C)(D)   4 (F)(G)(H)(J)   8 (F)(G)(H)(J)
B (F)(G)(H)(J)   5 (A)(B)(C)(D)   9 (A)(B)(C)(D)
1 (A)(B)(C)(D)   6 (F)(G)(H)(J)   10 (F)(G)(H)(J)
2 (F)(G)(H)(J)   C (A)(B)(C)(D)
3 (A)(B)(C)(D)   7 (A)(B)(C)(D)

1-57768-722-1 *Spectrum Test Practice 2*

LANGUAGE PRACTICE TEST

● Part 1: Listening

Directions: Read or listen carefully to the story and look at all of the pictures. Choose the best answer to each question.

Directions: Read these words. Which one is different from the other three?

Examples

A. Kyle went to the pet store. He really wanted a new puppy but his dad said he had to wait until he was twelve. Kyle was only eight. He was excited because he got to get a new pet. He had already gotten an underwater castle, pebbles, and a pump. What will Kyle buy?

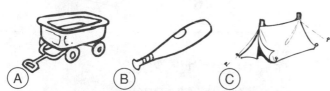
Ⓐ   Ⓑ   Ⓒ

B.
Ⓕ roof
Ⓖ door
Ⓗ window
Ⓙ road

---

1. Julia was excited to open her last birthday gift. She couldn't wait to use it in her next softball game. She knew what was in the box even before she opened it by the thin and long shape of it. What was Julia's last birthday gift?

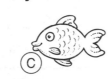
Ⓐ   Ⓑ   Ⓒ

2. The Wheeler family packed a lunch to eat in the park. Mom had a special surprise for them. She had baked something sweet and yummy. It was even Dad's favorite kind, blueberry. What was Mom's surprise for the family?

Ⓕ   Ⓖ   Ⓗ

3.
Ⓐ butterfly
Ⓑ mouse
Ⓒ ant
Ⓓ spider

4.
Ⓕ September
Ⓖ October
Ⓗ July
Ⓙ November

5.
Ⓐ rowboat
Ⓑ canoe
Ⓒ sailboat
Ⓓ car

STOP

LANGUAGE PRACTICE TEST

● **Part 2: Language Mechanics**

Directions: Read the sentences. Choose the best answer.

Examples

What sentence is capitalized and punctuated correctly?
 	
A.   Ⓐ The month of November has 31 days.
      Ⓑ When is mary's birthday!
      Ⓒ In July, i have my birthday?
	Read the following. Look at the underlined part. Which corrections does it need?
	
	B.
	
	Penny Gunter
	37 Page Avenue
	grand haven colorado 55889
	
	   Ⓕ Grand Haven colorado 55889
	   Ⓖ Grand haven, Colorado 55889
	   Ⓗ Grand Haven, Colorado 55889

Choose the sentence with no errors.

1.   Ⓐ The state of arizona is very hot and dry.
     Ⓑ America celebrates Thanksgiving in November.
     Ⓒ brian, put on your shoes?

2.   Ⓕ Brett plays soccer for Saranac Elementary School.
     Ⓖ My team, the bears, bought new Shirts to wear.
     Ⓗ Why did your dad say you were leaving in may?

3.   Ⓐ Go home, sally!
     Ⓑ Did your brother dave go with you?
     Ⓒ They went on vacation to Mt. Rushmore.

_____ (4)
_____ (5)
     There was a spelling bee at school. Guess what? I won! I spelled the word caramel. It was very exciting.
_____ (6)

4.   Ⓕ march 15 2002
     Ⓖ March 15, 2002
     Ⓗ March 5 2002

5.   Ⓐ Dear Grandma,
     Ⓑ Dear Grandma
     Ⓒ Dear grandma,

6.   Ⓕ love
     Ⓖ Love,
     Ⓗ love,

GO ON

Name _____ Date _____

● **Part 2: Language Mechanics (cont.)**

Directions: Read the story. Look at the underlined part. Choose the answer that shows the correct capitalization and punctuation.

Examples

Camp ends in a few <u>weeks i</u> had fun swimming, riding horses, and playing with
    (C)

my <u>friends chris</u> and I are happy to be coming home.
    (D)

C.   Ⓐ   weeks? i   **D.**   Ⓕ   friends! Chris

        Ⓑ   weeks. I   Ⓖ   friends, chris

        Ⓒ   week's. i   Ⓗ   Friends. Chris

On the Fourth of <u>july! my</u> family and I go to our cottage. Our cottage is on
    (7)

<u>Bills lake. we</u> watch fireworks, eat lunch, go swimming, and vote for our favorite
    (8)

boat in the boat parade.

7.   Ⓐ   July. My   **8.**   Ⓕ   Bill's Lake. We

       Ⓑ   July? my   Ⓖ   Bill's lake. we

       Ⓒ   July, my   Ⓗ   Bills lake. We

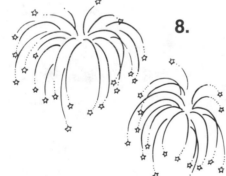

It is <u>dennys birthday</u> on <u>may 23. i wont</u> be able to see him on his special day.
    (9)   **(10)**

Even though I can't be there, I hope all his birthday wishes come true.

9.   Ⓐ   Denny's birthday   **10.**   Ⓕ   May 23. I won't

       Ⓑ   denny's Birthday   Ⓖ   may 23. I won't

       Ⓒ   Denny's Birthday   Ⓗ   May 23. i wont'

STOP

Name _____   Date _____

LANGUAGE PRACTICE TEST

● **Part 3: Language Expression**

Directions: Look at the sentence. What word or phrase fits in the blank or should be substituted for the underlined part?

Examples

A. The math test was the _____ he had ever taken.

- Ⓐ easy
- Ⓑ easiest
- Ⓒ easily
- Ⓓ easier

B. <u>Lynn</u> was very frightened by the movie.

- Ⓕ it
- Ⓖ she
- Ⓗ her
- Ⓙ there

---

1. My grandma's house is _____ than our house.

- Ⓐ big
- Ⓑ nice
- Ⓒ bigger
- Ⓓ biggest

2. Mom always used to_____ my sandwiches for me.

- Ⓕ cut
- Ⓖ cutted
- Ⓗ cuts
- Ⓙ cutting

3. All of the _____ are going to new homes tomorrow.

- Ⓐ cat
- Ⓑ kitty
- Ⓒ kitten
- Ⓓ kittens

4. <u>Tim and Eddy</u> are getting a new dog.

- Ⓕ them
- Ⓖ us
- Ⓗ he
- Ⓙ they

5. <u>The tree house</u> was old and was almost falling down.

- Ⓐ There
- Ⓑ Them
- Ⓒ It
- Ⓓ He

6. Will you pick up <u>your sister</u> from school?

- Ⓕ her
- Ⓖ we
- Ⓗ him
- Ⓙ it

Name _____   Date_____

● Part 3: Language Expression (cont.)

Directions: Read the sentences. Which one is <u>not</u> correct? Example C has been done for you.

Example

C.

(A) My birthday are in October.

(B) I love it in the fall

(C) when all the leaves change color.

7. (A) Marty and her grandpa
    (B) love to go fishing.
    (C) They are five lakes in their county.

8. (F) Last fall it wasn't not very warm.
    (G) Grandpa and I wore sweaters
    (H) every day when we fished.

9. (A) I didn't catch very many fish,
    (B) but Grandpa catched a lot.
    (C) He took home almost 20 fish!

10. (F) Dorothy found a box
    (G) at her grandma's house.
    (H) The box held lot of toy car.

11. (A) She never not dumped the cars out on the floor.
    (B) Dorothy picked one out at a time.
    (C) She placed them in a straight line.

12. (F) After the cars were out of the box,
    (G) Dorothy turn the box over
    (H) and made it into a garage.

GO ON

LANGUAGE PRACTICE TEST

● **Part 3: Language Expression (cont.)**

Directions: Read the sentence. What phrase should fit in the blank?

Example

D. **In May we plant our garden _____.**

  ⒡ leaving the clouds in the sky.
  ⒢ June it will grow.
  ⒣ went to my granddad's house.
  ⒥ with lots of vegetables.

13. **The train blew its whistle as it _____.**

  Ⓐ to go around in circles.
  Ⓑ passed through the town.
  Ⓒ for very fast tracks.
  Ⓓ talking to my dad.

14. **Please bring the book _____ to the library.**

  ⒡ leaving me
  ⒢ in the dark
  ⒣ that is overdue
  ⒥ smiling and laughing

15. **There are _____ eggs in the nest.**

  Ⓐ many blue speckled
  Ⓑ so they break
  Ⓒ mommy bird fed her babies
  Ⓓ baby tigers drink milk

16. **Ted has a bad cold and does not feel _____.**

  ⒡ leaving his socks out.
  ⒢ soup is good.
  ⒣ like eating dinner.
  ⒥ around the house.

17. **Betsy wrote the letter _____ with special colored markers.**

  Ⓐ grabbing a pen
  Ⓑ to her pen pal
  Ⓒ the pretty paper
  Ⓓ over the moon

18. **The puppy ran _____ and got all wet.**

  ⒡ barks a lot
  ⒢ eats his dog treats
  ⒣ through the sprinkler
  ⒥ treating us to ice cream

GO ON

Name _____ Date _____

LANGUAGE PRACTICE TEST

● **Part 3: Language Expression (cont.)**

Directions: Read the sentence. Which one is a complete sentence?

Example

E.
- (A) Downtown to get nice dinner.
- (B) The Jared family new black car.
- (C) Go home if you are sick.
- (D) Why he leaving the party?

19.
- (A) Five children are on the team.
- (B) Basketball with her cousins.
- (C) The storm was so.
- (D) Red and black checkers.

22.
- (F) The car down the street.
- (G) Brad was mad.
- (H) When it chewed his mitt.
- (J) Home in the rain.

20.
- (F) That old rag to wipe off your boots.
- (G) The clerk took the box away.
- (H) In the rain and in the snow.
- (J) The car almost out of gas.

23.
- (A) In the front row of the theater.
- (B) The boys with the green jackets.
- (C) Do the new shoes fit you?
- (D) Wants his friend to contest.

21.
- (A) Prize for baking the pie.
- (B) Dirt off your hands.
- (C) Jump up and wag its tail.
- (D) There was no light.

24.
- (F) I threw a ball.
- (G) Over the fence and through the window.
- (H) The broken toy on the steps.
- (J) The trail to the top of the mountain.

GO ON

1-57768-722-1 *Spectrum Test Practice 2*

LANGUAGE PRACTICE TEST

● **Part 3: Language Expression (cont.)**

Directions: Read the paragraph. Which choice best fits in the blank?

Example

F.   **Monty is a good boy. _____ His mother is grateful he knows it is important to listen.**

   (F)   Dad says he can go out to play.

   (G)   The castle over the hill has a princess that lives in it.

   (H)   Monty's favorite thing to do is go to parades.

   (J)   He wants to be a good listener.

25.   **_____ They like baseball, basketball, and tennis.**

   (A)   Joel and Tony love sports.

   (B)   Joel and Tony like running.

   (C)   Joel and Tony love to eat candy.

   (D)   Joel and Tony like to swim.

26.   **The class went to the library to check out books. They also learned about the library and library skills. _____**

   (F)   The books were overdue.

   (G)   The librarian taught them a lot.

   (H)   The teacher graded the paper.

   (J)   The children left school.

27.   **Julie imagined herself on the wings of a large bird flying _____.**

   (A)   up on the top of his feather.

   (B)   running up the hill.

   (C)   through the clouds.

   (D)   clouds in the sky.

28. **The trip to the jungle was _____.**

   (F)   leaving many animals without homes.

   (G)   many trees were being cut down.

   (H)   going to happen in the next two months.

   (J)   needing to eat lunch.

29. **While looking _____, I called her name. I was upset she was lost.**

   (A)   nearing the garage

   (B)   driving down the street

   (C)   for my lost cat

   (D)   cutting off her collar

30. **The pie_____was cooling. It was for the party later that day.**

   (F)   imagines it was dreaming

   (G)   inside the dog

   (H)   around the neighborhood

   (J)   sitting on the windowsill

GO ON

Name _____ Date _____

● **Part 3: Language Expression (cont.)**

Directions: Read the paragraph. Answer the questions that follow.

Example

Betsy got a new pail and shovel to build sand castles. She also got a new towel and an umbrella for the beach. Her mom was going to get her a bathing suit too.

G. **Which sentence does not belong in the paragraph?**

(A) Betsy thought she should get some sun tan lotion.

(B) Betsy got a new beach hat.

(C) Betsy did a good job on her math test.

Giraffes are the tallest animals. They have long necks and long legs. They live on the grasslands in Africa. Giraffes live in small groups called herds. A giraffe uses its long tongue to grab leaves from tall tree branches. To drink, a giraffe must spread its front legs apart and lower its head. Then it can reach the water.

31. **Which sentence does not belong in this paragraph?**

(A) Africa has many animals living there.

(B) A giraffe seldom uses its voice.

(C) A giraffe's hair is short.

32. **Which sentence does belong in this paragraph?**

(F) Tall trees are good to have in forests.

(G) A giraffe's hair is colored with reddish-brown spots.

(H) You can find a lot of animals at watering holes.

33. **Juan was asked to write a second paragraph after the one above. His paragraph was about enemies of the giraffe. What did he do before he wrote his paragraph?**

(A) thought about whom he doesn't like

(B) wrote a list of all the enemies of the giraffe

(C) called his Aunt Terri and asked her how to help giraffes

34. **What should the topic of Juan's second paragraph be?**

(F) enemies of the giraffe

(G) how giraffes look

(H) lions and where they live

LANGUAGE PRACTICE TEST

● **Part 3: Language Expression (cont.)**

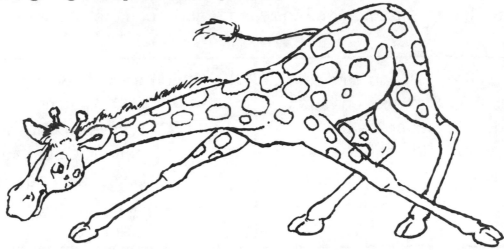

35. What sentence could Juan use to begin the second paragraph?

- Ⓐ Even though many people enjoy looking at the giraffe, it has many enemies.
- Ⓑ The enemies of the world try to hurt nature.
- Ⓒ My brother's favorite animal is the giraffe too.

36. What would be a good sentence to end the second paragraph?

- Ⓕ Giraffes are fun to watch.
- Ⓖ As you can see, the giraffe has many enemies.
- Ⓗ Another enemy can sometimes be people.

37. Where might Juan look to find information about the giraffe's enemies?

- Ⓐ at the pet store
- Ⓑ in a dictionary
- Ⓒ at the library

38. What would be a good topic for a third paragraph?

- Ⓕ what life is like in a giraffe herd
- Ⓖ where elephants live
- Ⓗ how Africa would be a cool place to visit

39. Which sentence would belong in the third paragraph?

- Ⓐ Giraffes have very long legs.
- Ⓑ Giraffes have tails.
- Ⓒ Giraffes live together in small groups called herds.
- Ⓓ Lions really want to be nice to giraffes.

1-57768-722-1 *Spectrum Test Practice 2*

Name _____   Date_____

● Part 4: Spelling

Directions: Which word fits in the blank and is spelled correctly?

> **Example**
>
> A.   He has left for school _____.
>
>   (A) already
>
>   (B) allredy
>
>   (C) alredy
>
>   (D) allreedy

1.   She _____ the corner too quickly.

    (A) trned

    (B) tirned

    (C) turned

    (D) terned

2.   Wait _____ we get to the hotel.

    (F) unntil

    (G) untille

    (H) untill

    (J) until

3.   She is _____ a good time with her friends.

    (A) haveing

    (B) having

    (C) haeving

    (D) halfing

4.   Her grades were very _____ to her.

    (F) important

    (G) inporant

    (H) importent

    (J) inpoortant

5.   Quick, _____ the ball to Ted!

    (A) throw

    (B) throh

    (C) throo

    (D) throuw

6.   There were _____ winners of the contest.

    (F) threee

    (G) threa

    (H) thre

    (J) three

GO ON

1-57768-722-1 *Spectrum Test Practice 2*

LANGUAGE PRACTICE TEST

● **Part 4: Spelling (cont.)**

Directions: Find the words that are <u>not</u> spelled correctly.

Examples

Which word in each group is <u>not</u> spelled correctly?	**Read the sentences. Which underlined word is <u>not</u> spelled correctly?**
B. Ⓕ allthough 　　Ⓖ anything 　　Ⓗ build 　　Ⓙ can't	**C.** <u>Dering</u> the <u>storm</u> three trees 　　　Ⓐ　　　　　Ⓑ 　　<u>blew</u> over. 　　Ⓒ

---

7. Ⓐ find
　　Ⓑ give
　　Ⓒ fineally
　　Ⓓ family

8. Ⓕ hard
　　Ⓖ happe
　　Ⓗ kept
　　Ⓙ large

9. Ⓐ anumal
　　Ⓑ everything
　　Ⓒ it's
　　Ⓓ instead

10. She <u>guessed</u> the <u>correct</u> <u>numbr</u>.
　　　　　　Ⓕ　　　　　Ⓖ　　　Ⓗ

11. Were <u>thay</u> going to be <u>able</u> to get
　　　　　　Ⓐ　　　　　　　　Ⓑ

　　the <u>money</u>?
　　　　Ⓒ

12. The cat <u>chasing</u> the dog was an
　　　　　　　　Ⓕ

　　<u>amazing</u> <u>sigt</u>!
　　Ⓖ　　　Ⓗ

STOP

LANGUAGE PRACTICE TEST

● Part 5: Study Skills

Directions: Read the questions. Choose the correct answer.

Examples

This is from a book about mammals.

Table of Contents	
Introduction	1
Bears	4
The Feline or Cat Family	22
The Canine or Dog Family	38
Dolphins	52
More Mammals in the Water	70
Index	82
Glossary	91

A. Where can you learn about beavers?

- (A) pages 22–37
- (B) pages 70–81
- (C) pages 1–3
- (D) pages 82–90

B. Which set is in alphabetical order?

- (F) fast, leave, dry, page
- (G) leave, fast, dry, page
- (H) page, leave, fast, dry
- (J) dry, fast, leave, page

Use the table of contents above to answer questions 1–3.

1. If you're not sure if otters are in the book, where should you look?

- (A) index
- (B) introduction
- (C) page 5
- (D) glossary

2. Where can you learn about tigers?

- (F) pages 22–37
- (G) in the glossary
- (H) in the index
- (J) in the introduction

3. Where can Jo learn about dolphins?

- (A) pages 2–15
- (B) pages 16–24
- (C) pages 52–69
- (D) pages 38–51

4. Which set is in alphabetical order?

- (F) across, heart, hill, sky
- (G) heart, hill, sky, across
- (H) across, hill, heart, sky
- (J) sky, hill, heart, across

5. If the guide words are people—possible, which word could you find on the dictionary page?

- (A) page
- (B) party
- (C) problem
- (D) plants

6. Nan wants the names in alphabetical order: Kat, Lori, Ang, Ema, and Mike. Who comes after Kat?

- (F) Ang
- (G) Ema
- (H) Mike
- (J) Lori

GO ON

LANGUAGE PRACTICE TEST

● **Part 5: Study Skills (cont.)**

Directions: Read the map. Choose the best answer.

Example

C. On what street do you find the police station?

  (A) Adams Street
  (B) Second Street
  (C) Cedar Street
  (D) Depot Street

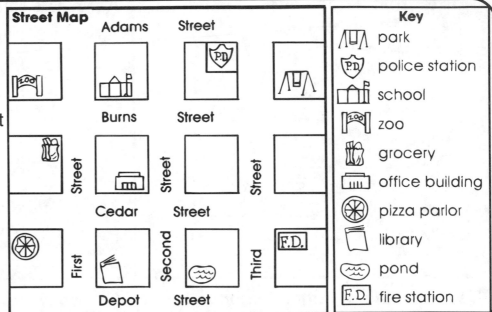

7. A class is on a field trip at the fire station. Which direction do they need to go in order to get to the park?

  (A) north
  (B) south
  (C) east
  (D) west

8. What is at the corner of First Street and Burns Street?

  (F) zoo
  (G) grocery
  (H) office building
  (J) school

9. Mrs. Swanson is at the library with her two children. She wants to take them to the park next. Which direction should she go and which street should she take to get there the quickest?

  (A) south on First Street
  (B) south on Third Street
  (C) east on Depot Street
  (D) west on Cedar Street

10. Hunter lives on Burns Street next to the school and wants to go to Depot Street. Which direction must he travel?

  (F) north
  (G) south
  (H) east
  (J) west

102

Name _____ Date_____

MATH: CONCEPTS

● Lesson 1: Numeration

Directions: Read or listen to the question. Then choose the best answer.

Example

A. How many are there?

   (A) 43
   (B) 68
   (C) 51
   (D) 57

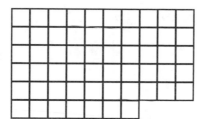

 Clue Read or listen carefully to the problem and think about what to do before you choose an answer.

● Practice

1. Which squares contain numbers that are all less than 19?

   (A) 7 15 10 18
   (B) 91 20 32 57
   (C) 18 6 23 65
   (D) 12 81 17 44

2. Which numbers should go in the blank spaces when you count by ones?

   38, 39,_____, 41, 42, 43, _____

   (F) 40 and 44
   (G) 29 and 45
   (H) 30 and 46
   (J) 39 and 44

3. Which shape is fifth from the star?

   (A)

   (B) △

   (C)

   (D) ○

4. Which number is the expanded numeral for seven hundred eighty-six?

   (F) 60 + 80+ 70
   (G) 70 + 80 + 60
   (H) 700 + 80 + 6
   (J) 70 + 86

1-57768-722-1 *Spectrum Test Practice 2*

● **Lesson 1: Numeration (cont.)**

5. There are 57 unbaked cookies on the counter. Each pan will hold ten cookies. How many pans can be filled completely with cookies?

    (A) 7

    (B) 5

    (C) 10

    (D) 6

6. Which numeral should replace the circle on the number line?

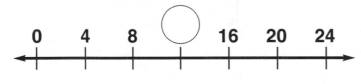

    (F) 11

    (G) 12

    (H) 15

    (J) 10

7. Which numeral shows the difference between 5 and 12?

    (A) 7

    (B) 9

    (C) 6

    (D) 5

8. Which group of numbers is in the correct counting order?

    (F) 79, 78, 77, 80, 81

    (G) 78, 79, 77, 80, 81

    (H) 77, 78, 79, 80, 81

    (J) 79, 77, 78, 81, 80

9. Look at the flowers. Which group of base 10 blocks has the same number as the flowers?

(A)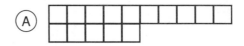

(B)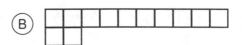

(C)

(D)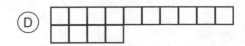

STOP

1-57768-722-1 *Spectrum Test Practice 2*

Name _____   Date _____

● **Lesson 2: Number Concepts**

Directions: Read or listen to the question. Then choose the best answer.

╭─── **Example** ───╮

A. **Which numeral matches the word?**

┌─────────────────────┐
│   **seventy**   │
└─────────────────────┘

Ⓐ 7
Ⓑ 17
Ⓒ 77
Ⓓ 70

 Clue Look at all the answer choices before you mark the one you think is correct.

● **Practice**

1. **Which number word goes in the blank in the box?**

┌────────────────────────────────┐
│ ten, eleven, _____, thirteen │
└────────────────────────────────┘

Ⓐ fifteen
Ⓑ twelve
Ⓒ nine
Ⓓ fourteen

2. **Which number is seven hundred thirty-five?**

Ⓕ 735
Ⓖ 7035
Ⓗ 7305
Ⓙ 739

3. **Which number matches the words in the box?**

┌────────────────────────────────┐
│ five thousand three hundred   │
└────────────────────────────────┘

Ⓐ 30,500
Ⓑ 3,005
Ⓒ 5,300
Ⓓ 53

4. **Which number matches the number in the middle of the box?**

┌────────────────────────────────┐
│ **11, 12, 13, 14, 15**   │
└────────────────────────────────┘

Ⓕ eleven
Ⓖ thirteen
Ⓗ fifteen
Ⓙ twelve

 GO ON

● **Lesson 2: Number Concepts (cont.)**

5. **Which number is two hundred sixty-one?**

   (A) 216
   (B) 261
   (C) 2061
   (D) 2601

6. **Which number matches the word in the box?**

   | five hundred sixteen |

   (F) 561
   (G) 500,016
   (H) 5016
   (J) 516

7. **Which number is three-thousand four-hundred fifty?**

   (A) 30,450
   (B) 3,450
   (C) 3540
   (D) 3054

8. **Which word stands for the number in the box?**

   | 43 |

   (F) thirty-four
   (G) forty
   (H) forty-three
   (J) forty-four

9. **If you are counting by ones, which number word should go in the box?**

   | twenty-nine, _____, thirty-one, thirty-two |

   (A) thirty
   (B) forty
   (C) fifty
   (D) twenty-eight

STOP

Name _____   Date _____

● **Lesson 3: Patterns and Place Value**

Directions: Read or listen to the question. Then choose the best answer.

Example

A. Which pattern shows counting by threes?

- (A) 3, 5, 8
- (B) 2, 4, 8
- (C) 9, 10, 11
- (D) 6, 9, 12

Clue If you are not sure which answer choice is correct, take your best guess.

● **Practice**

1. Look at the hundreds, tens, and ones chart. Which number is represented by the dots on the chart?

100s	10s	1s
•• •• •• ••	•• ••	•• •• •• •

- (A) 756
- (B) 857
- (C) 847
- (D) 846

2. Which digit is in the hundreds place?

4016

- (F) 4
- (G) 0
- (H) 1
- (J) 6

3. Which shape is one-third shaded?

(A)

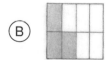
(B)

(C)

(D)

GO ON

MATH: CONCEPTS

● **Lesson 3: Patterns and Place Value (cont.)**

4. **Which number is missing from the pattern?**

   (F) 6
   (G) 8
   (H) 9
   (J) 10

5. **Look at the pattern. Which shape below should come next in the pattern?**

   (A) ○
   (B) □
   (C) △
   (D) ▭

6. **Which number in the box does not belong?**

   12, 16, 18, 20, 24, 28

   (F) 18
   (G) 20
   (H) 24
   (J) 12

7. **Which is the place value of the number 4?**

   945

   (A) ones
   (B) tens
   (C) hundreds

8. **Which number has 6 ones and 3 hundreds?**

   (F) 563
   (G) 653
   (H) 356
   (J) 536

STOP

MATH: CONCEPTS

Lesson 4: Properties

Directions: Read or listen to the question. Then choose the best answer.

Example

A. Look at the number sentence in the box. Which sign will make the sentence true?

(A) ÷
(B) x
(C) +
(D) −

$$8\ \square\ 3 = 5$$

 Clue Look carefully at the answer choices. Be sure you fill in the space next to the one you think is correct.

Practice

1. How many problems have an answer equal to four?

7	8	9	2	1
+ 3	− 4	− 6	+ 2	+ 3

(A) 4
(B) 1
(C) 5
(D) 3

2. Which multiplication fact is shown by the dots?

(F) 3 x 4 = 12
(G) 3 x 6 = 18
(H) 4 x 4 = 16
(J) 2 x 9 = 18

3. Which group of number statements equals the same as the word in the box?

eight

(A) 10 − 5
     3 + 2

(B) 4 + 4
     11 − 3

(C) 13 − 6
     4 + 3

(D) 8 + 3
     15 − 4

GO ON

MATH: CONCEPTS

● **Lesson 4: Properties (cont.)**

4. Which means the same as 4 is less than 10?

- Ⓕ 4 = 10
- Ⓖ 10 + 4
- Ⓗ 4 > 10
- Ⓙ 10 > 4

6. Which number is thirty-one rounded to the nearest ten?

- Ⓕ 10
- Ⓖ 30
- Ⓗ 40
- Ⓙ 50

5. Five ants live in the colony. Four leave the colony. Which number sentence shows how many ants are left in the colony?

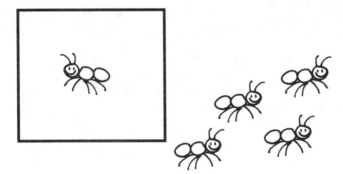

- Ⓐ 5 − 4 = 1
- Ⓑ 5 + 4 = 9
- Ⓒ 9 − 5 = 4
- Ⓓ 6 + 4 = 10

7. Look at the number sentence in the box. Which number is the best estimate of your answer?

$$276 + 88 = \square$$

- Ⓐ 100
- Ⓑ 600
- Ⓒ 200
- Ⓓ 350

STO

1-57768-722-1 *Spectrum Test Practice*

Name _____   Date_____

MATH: CONCEPTS
SAMPLE TEST

● **Directions:** Read or listen to the question. Then choose the best answer.

Example

A. Fifteen students are in a lunch line. Emma is fifth in line. How many students are behind Emma?

- (A) 7
- (B) 21
- (C) 10
- (D) 14

---

1. Look at the shapes. Which fraction tells what part of the shapes are triangles?

- (A) $\frac{2}{3}$
- (B) $\frac{1}{4}$
- (C) $\frac{3}{4}$
- (D) $\frac{1}{2}$

2. Which answer shows how many tens and ones are in fifty-seven?

- (F) 7 tens and 5 ones
- (G) 3 tens and 7 ones
- (H) 5 tens and 4 ones
- (J) 5 tens and 7 ones

3. Which number matches the base ten blocks?

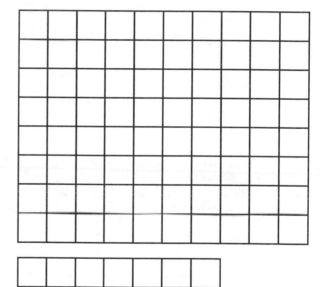

- (A) 47
- (B) 87
- (C) 78
- (D) 32

GO ON

1-57768-722-1 *Spectrum Test Practice 2*

MATH: CONCEPTS
SAMPLE TEST (cont.)

4. Which number is shown in the chart below?

100s	10s	1s
●●	●● ●● ●	●● ●● ●● ●● ●

- (F) 592
- (G) 259
- (H) 952
- (J) 148

5. What numeral should replace the square?

5   10   15   ☐   25   30

- (A) 18
- (B) 20
- (C) 23
- (D) 18

6. Which number matches the word in the box?

> ## nine hundred thirteen

- (F) 9,013
- (G) 9,413
- (H) 913
- (J) 3391

7. Which numeral means one hundred, five tens, eight ones?

- (A) 158
- (B) 1,058
- (C) 581
- (D) 815

8. Which numeral is between 59 and 88?

- (F) 40
- (G) 57
- (H) 91
- (J) 60

GO ON

1-57768-722-1 *Spectrum Test Practice 2*

9. **Which number should go in each box to make both sentences true?**

$$9 + \square = 16$$

$$16 - \square = 9$$

- Ⓐ 7
- Ⓑ 8
- Ⓒ 9
- Ⓓ 10

10. **Look at the pattern. Which shape below should come next in the pattern?**

- Ⓕ ◯
- Ⓖ ▢
- Ⓗ ▲
- Ⓙ △

11. **Which means the same as 15 is less than 25?**
- Ⓐ 25 − 15
- Ⓑ 15 > 25
- Ⓒ 25 < 15
- Ⓓ 25 > 15

GO ON

12. There are 86 children going on the field trip. Each bus holds ten children. How many buses will be filled completely?

- (F) 6
- (G) 7
- (H) 8
- (J) 9

13. How many problems below have the answer of twelve?

$$15 - 5 = \square$$

$$12 - 0 = \square$$

$$6 + 7 = \square$$

$$4 + 8 = \square$$

$$9 + 4 = \square$$

- (A) 1
- (B) 2
- (C) 3
- (D) 4

14. Which symbol is needed to make the number sentence true?

$$8 + 6 = 18 \;\square\; 4$$

- (F) +
- (G) −
- (H) x
- (J) ÷

15. Which number is missing?

$$3, 9, \underline{\hspace{1cm}}, 21, 27$$

- (A) 12
- (B) 15
- (C) 18
- (D) 20

STOP

Name _____ Date _____

MATH: COMPUTATION

Lesson 5: Addition

Directions: Solve each addition problem. Choose the best answer.

Examples

This one has been done for you.	Practice on this one.

A.   8
      + 2

Ⓐ 11
Ⓑ 9
Ⓒ 12
 10

B.   15
      + 3

Ⓕ 17
Ⓖ 16
Ⓗ 18
Ⓙ 19

Clue If a problem is too difficult, skip it and come back to it later if you have time.

Practice

1.   33
      + 5

Ⓐ 54
Ⓑ 60
Ⓒ 38
Ⓓ 58

3. 502 + 26 = ☐

Ⓐ 482
Ⓑ 628
Ⓒ 528
Ⓓ 608

2. 34 + 41 = ☐

Ⓕ 75
Ⓖ 65
Ⓗ 77
Ⓙ 85

4.   11
       5
      + 2

Ⓕ 16
Ⓖ 15
Ⓗ 19
Ⓙ 18

GO ON

1-57768-722-1 *Spectrum Test Practice 2*

MATH: COMPUTATION

● **Lesson 5: Addition (cont.)**

5.
$$
\begin{array}{r}
342 \\
+\ 497 \\
\end{array}
$$

- (A) 839
- (B) 939
- (C) 844
- (D) 838

8.
$$
\begin{array}{r}
8 \\
+\ 6 \\
\end{array}
$$

- (F) 14
- (G) 16
- (H) 12
- (J) 15

6. $17 + 31 = \square$

- (F) 47
- (G) 48
- (H) 58
- (J) 85

9.
$$
\begin{array}{r}
7 \\
+\ 26 \\
\end{array}
$$

- (A) 34
- (B) 44
- (C) 33
- (D) 32

7. $8 + 4 + 7 = \square$

- (A) 17
- (B) 20
- (C) 19
- (D) 29

10.
$$
\begin{array}{r}
11 \\
68 \\
+\ 15 \\
\end{array}
$$

- (F) 101
- (G) 96
- (H) 84
- (J) 94

STO

MATH: COMPUTATION

● Lesson 6: Subtraction

Directions: Solve each subtraction problem. Choose the best answer.

Examples

This one has been done for you.	Practice on this one.

A.   12
     − 5
 	
 Ⓐ 7 (crossed out)
 Ⓑ 10
 Ⓒ 8
 Ⓓ 4
	B. 18
	     − 4
	
	 Ⓕ 13
	 Ⓖ 16
	 Ⓗ 14
	 Ⓙ 15

Clue If you cannot find the answer to a problem, take your best guess and move on to the next problem.

● Practice

1.   49
     − 23
- Ⓐ 52
- Ⓑ 26
- Ⓒ 36
- Ⓓ 62

3.   355 − 78 = □
- Ⓐ 177
- Ⓑ 279
- Ⓒ 277
- Ⓓ 79

2.   26 − 5 = □
- Ⓕ 21
- Ⓖ 31
- Ⓗ 20
- Ⓙ 22

4.   66 − 49 = □
- Ⓕ 27
- Ⓖ 17
- Ⓗ 19
- Ⓙ 18

GO ON

MATH: COMPUTATION

● Lesson 6: Subtraction (cont.)

5. 253
   − 74

(A) 279
(B) 176
(C) 179
(D) 163

8. 586
   − 98

(F) 488
(G) 589
(H) 482
(J) 478

6. 68¢
   − 21¢

(F) 57¢
(G) 47¢
(H) 48¢
(J) 49¢

9. 365 − 76 = □

(A) 281
(B) 279
(C) 289
(D) 441

7. 7 − 4 = □

(A) 2
(B) 3
(C) 4
(D) 5

10. 923
    − 567

(F) 1490
(G) 456
(H) 445
(J) 356

STOP

1-57768-722-1 Spectrum Test Practice 2

Name_____ Date_____

● Lesson 7: Multiplication and Division

Directions: Solve these multiplication and division problems. Choose the best answer.

Examples

This one has been done for you.	Practice on this one.
A. $\begin{array}{r} 2 \\ \times\ 7 \\ \hline \end{array}$ (A) 12 (B) 14 (C) 11 (D) 10	B. $9 \div 3 = \square$ (F) 3 (G) 2 (H) 1 (J) 6

 Clue Look carefully at the problem to be sure you are performing the correct operation.

● Practice

1. $\begin{array}{r} 8 \\ \times\ 3 \\ \hline \end{array}$
   (A) 11
   (B) 5
   (C) 24
   (D) 21

3. $18 \div 6 = \square$
   (A) 24
   (B) 2
   (C) 3
   (D) 12

2. $2 \times 9 = \square$
   (F) 18
   (G) 16
   (H) 11
   (J) 7

4. $4\overline{)20}$
   (F) 5
   (G) 4
   (H) 16
   (J) 11

STOP

Name _____   Date _____

● **Directions:** Solve each problem. Choose the best answer.

Examples

This one has been done for you.		Practice on this one.	
A. 4 <u>+ 3</u>	Ⓐ 1 7 Ⓒ 6 Ⓓ 8	**B.** 11¢ <u>– 5¢</u>	Ⓕ 7¢ Ⓖ 6¢ Ⓗ 8¢ Ⓙ 9¢

If a problem is too difficult, skip it and come back to it later if you have time.

1.   8
   <u>+ 8</u>
Ⓐ 15
Ⓑ 16
Ⓒ 0
Ⓓ 14

3. 841 – 65 = ☐
Ⓐ 906
Ⓑ 73
Ⓒ 96
Ⓓ 776

2. 78 + 25 = ☐
Ⓕ 43
Ⓖ 13
Ⓗ 103
Ⓙ 114

4.   52
   <u>– 7</u>
Ⓕ 45
Ⓖ 35
Ⓗ 59
Ⓙ 48

GO ON

1-57768-722-1 *Spectrum Test Practice 2*

Name _____   Date_____

5. $7 + 4 + 9 + 2 = \square$
Ⓐ 21
Ⓑ 32
Ⓒ 22
Ⓓ 12

8. $\begin{array}{r} 5 \\ \times\ 3 \\ \hline \end{array}$
Ⓕ 25
Ⓖ 15
Ⓗ 20
Ⓙ 8

6. $\begin{array}{r} 85¢ \\ -\ 37¢ \\ \hline \end{array}$
Ⓕ 58¢
Ⓖ 48¢
Ⓗ 47¢
Ⓙ 92¢

9. $8 \times 6 = \square$
Ⓐ 40
Ⓑ 12
Ⓒ 15
Ⓓ 48

7. $\begin{array}{r} 50 \\ 14 \\ +\ 36 \\ \hline \end{array}$
Ⓐ 100
Ⓑ 110
Ⓒ 95
Ⓓ 98

10. $36 \div 6 = \square$
Ⓕ 6
Ⓖ 5
Ⓗ 42
Ⓙ 30

STOP

Name _____   Date _____

MATH: APPLICATIONS

● **Lesson 8: Geometry**

Directions: Listen to the questions. Choose the best answer to each question.

Example

A. Which picture looks the most like a rectangle?

 (A)    (B)    (C)    (D)

 Clue Use key words, pictures, and numbers to help you find the answer.

● **Practice**

1. Which figure has three corners?
   - (A) square
   - (B) rectangle
   - (C) triangle
   - (D) circle

2. How many sides does a rectangle have?
   - (F) 3
   - (G) 4
   - (H) 5
   - (J) 6

3. What is the name of this figure?

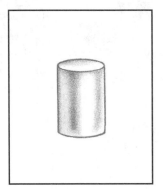

   - (A) sphere
   - (B) cone
   - (C) cylinder
   - (D) cube

GO ON

1-57768-722-1 *Spectrum Test Practice 2*

Name _____ Date _____

● **Lesson 8: Geometry (cont.)**

4. **Which shape would you have if you cut the book exactly in half?**

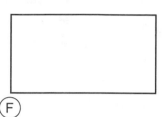 Ⓕ   Ⓖ   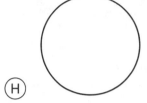 Ⓗ    Ⓙ

5. **How many of these shapes are cubes?**

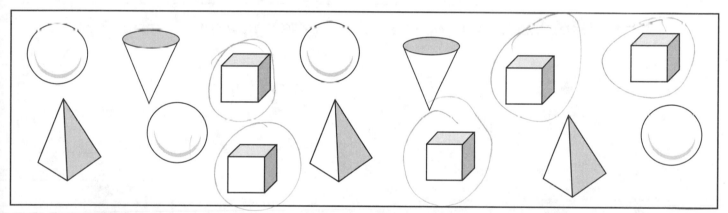

Ⓐ 2
Ⓑ 3
Ⓒ 4
Ⓓ 5

6. **What is the name of this figure?**
    Ⓕ cylinder
    Ⓖ cube
    Ⓗ sphere
    Ⓙ triangle

STOP

123   1-57768-722-1 *Spectrum Test Practice 2*

MATH: APPLICATIONS

● **Lesson 9: Geometry**

Directions: Listen to the questions. Choose the best answer to each question.

Example

A. **What is the perimeter of this figure?**

- Ⓐ 18 in.
- Ⓑ 9 in.
- Ⓒ 3 in.
- Ⓓ 27 in.

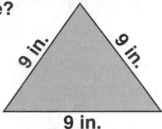

9 in.   9 in.

9 in.

Clue Use key words, pictures, and numbers to help you find the answer.

● **Practice**

1. **What shape would you have if you cut the egg exactly in half?**

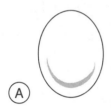   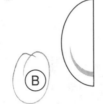

Ⓐ   Ⓑ   Ⓒ   Ⓓ

2. **Look at the figure in the box.**
   Which figure is the same size as the one in the box?

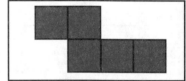

   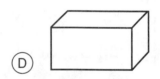

Ⓕ   Ⓖ   Ⓗ   Ⓙ

3. **Which figure's two sides will not match when it is folded?**

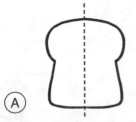   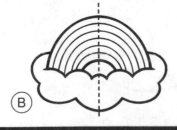   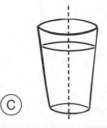   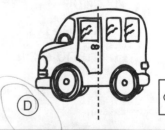

Ⓐ   Ⓑ   Ⓒ   Ⓓ

GO ON ➡

      1-57768-722-1 *Spectrum Test Practice 2*

● Lesson 9: Geometry (cont.)

4. **What is the perimeter of the figure?**

   F 20 in.

   G 8 in.

   H 40 in.

   J 28 in.

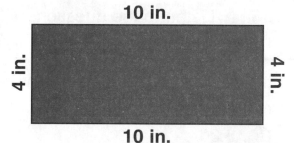
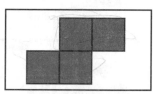

10 in.

4 in.   4 in.

10 in.

5. **Look at the figure in the box.
   Which figure is the same size as the one in the box?**

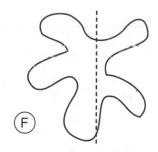

A

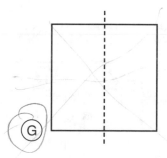

B

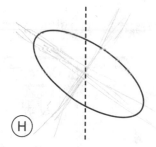

C

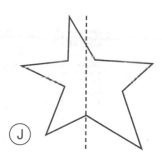

D

6. **If you fold one of these figures in half, two of the sides will match
   exactly. Which figure is it?**

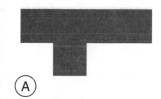

F   G   H   J

7. **What is the perimeter of the figure?**

   A 10 in.

   B 20 in.

   C 15 in.

   D 5 in.

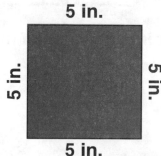

5 in.

5 in.   5 in.

5 in.

1-57768-722-1 *Spectrum Test Practice 2*

Name _____ Date _____

● **Lesson 10: Measurement**

Directions: Listen to the questions. Choose the best answer to each question.

Example

A. What time does the clock show?

- Ⓐ 5:15
- Ⓑ 6:30
- Ⓒ 5:45
- Ⓓ 6:40

 Clue If you work on scratch paper, be sure you copy numbers correctly and compute carefully.

● **Practice**

1. What time does the clock show?

- Ⓐ 9:15
- Ⓑ 10:30
- Ⓒ 11:45
- Ⓓ 11:15

2. Look at the calendars. In which month is the 17th on a Friday?

Sunday	Monday	Tuesday	Wednesday	Thursday	Friday	Saturday
			1	2	3	4
5	6	7	8	9	10	11
12	13	14	15	16	17	18
19	20	21	22	23	24	25
26	27	28	29	30	31	

Ⓕ

Sunday	Monday	Tuesday	Wednesday	Thursday	Friday	Saturday
		1	2	3	4	5
6	7	8	9	10	11	12
13	14	15	16	17	18	19
20	21	22	23	24	25	26
27	28	29	30			

Ⓖ

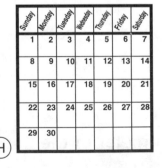

Sunday	Monday	Tuesday	Wednesday	Thursday	Friday	Saturday
1	2	3	4	5	6	7
8	9	10	11	12	13	14
15	16	17	18	19	20	21
22	23	24	25	26	27	28
29	30					

Ⓗ

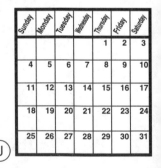

Sunday	Monday	Tuesday	Wednesday	Thursday	Friday	Saturday
					1	2	3
4	5	6	7	8	9	10
11	12	13	14	15	16	17
18	19	20	21	22	23	24
25	26	27	28	29	30	31

Ⓙ

3. Look at these coins. How much money do they show?

- Ⓐ 55¢
- Ⓑ 65¢
- Ⓒ 66¢
- Ⓓ 60¢

GO ON

MATH: APPLICATIONS

● **Lesson 10: Measurement (cont.)**

4. **Which number shows seven dollars and thirty-five cents?**

   (F) $7.35
   (G) $73.5
   (H) $.735
   (J) $735.

5. **Which object costs the most?**

   (A) $1.35   (B) $1.00   (C) $2.50   (D) $3.00

6. **Look at each clock. The first one shows what time the children went to the park. The second one shows what time they left the park. How long were they at the park?**

   (F) 2 hours
   (G) 20 minutes
   (H) 5 hours
   (J) 8 hours

7. **How much change would you get back if you bought something that cost a quarter and you paid for it with a dollar?**

   (A) 50¢
   (B) 75¢
   (C) 25¢
   (D) $1.00

8. **The time the clock shows is thirty minutes after what time?**

   (F) 6:00
   (G) 3:00
   (H) 8:00
   (J) 7:00

STOP

Name _____ Date _____

MATH: APPLICATIONS

● **Lesson 11: Measurement**

Directions: Listen to the questions. Choose the best answer to each question.

Example

A. **Which metric unit would be the best to use to show how long a car is?**

   Ⓐ gram
   Ⓑ liter
   Ⓒ kilometer
   Ⓓ meter

1. **Look at the objects. Which object might weigh ten pounds?**

Ⓐ   Ⓑ   Ⓒ   Ⓓ

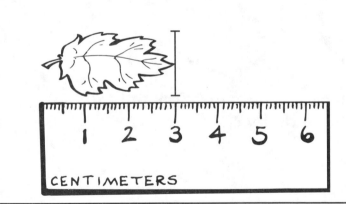 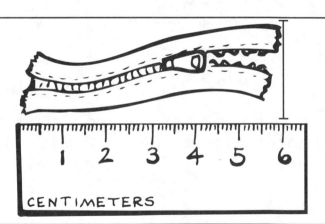

2. **Look at the rulers and the items pictured. What is the difference in length between the leaf and the zipper?**

   Ⓕ 3 cm
   Ⓖ 5 cm
   Ⓗ 13 cm
   Ⓙ 15 cm

3. **How long are the leaf and zipper if you put them together?**

   Ⓐ 5 cm
   Ⓑ 7 cm
   Ⓒ 9 cm
   Ⓓ 11 cm

GO ON

MATH: APPLICATIONS

● **Lesson 11: Measurement (cont.)**

4. **Which thermometer shows the temperature on a hot summer day?**

   (F) thermometer 1
   (G) thermometer 2
   (H) thermometer 3
   (J) thermometer 4

5. **Which thermometer shows the temperature on a cold winter day?**

   (A) thermometer 1
   (B) thermometer 2
   (C) thermometer 3
   (D) thermometer 4

1 **2** **3** **4**

6. **Which one of these objects is about an inch long in real life?**

 (F) (G)  (H)  (J)

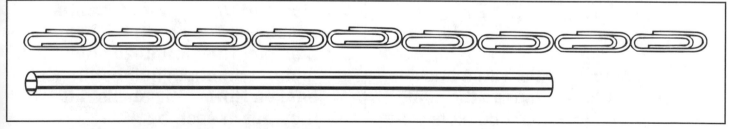

7. **How many paper clips long is the drinking straw?**

   (A) 10 paper clips
   (B) 4 paper clips
   (C) 20 paper clips
   (D) 7 paper clips

STOP

Name _____   Date _____

MATH: APPLICATIONS

● **Lesson 12: Problem Solving**

Directions: Listen to your teacher read each story problem.
Choose the best answer.

Example

A. Paula's pizza was $\frac{1}{2}$ cheese. The rest was sausage.
How much of the pizza was sausage?

- (A) $\frac{1}{2}$
- (B) $\frac{1}{3}$
- (C) $\frac{1}{4}$
- (D) the whole pizza

 Clue — Listen to the whole problem and think about what you should do before you choose an answer.

● **Practice**

1. Danny's sand castle took 9 buckets of sand to build. Gail's took 3 more buckets than Danny's. How many buckets of sand did it take to make Gail's castle?

   - (A) 8
   - (B) 12
   - (C) 14
   - (D) 3

2. Meg built a castle with 8 buckets of sand. Yolanda used the same amount. How many buckets were used altogether for the 2 castles?

   - (F) 20
   - (G) 8
   - (H) 16
   - (J) 14

3. Next, all the children built a huge castle with 13 rooms. A wave washed away 5 of the rooms. How many rooms were left?

   - (A) 2
   - (B) 4
   - (C) 6
   - (D) 8

4. Meg and Danny went to gather seashells. They each had two buckets. They found 20 shells and put an equal number in each bucket. How many shells did they put in each bucket?

   - (F) 3
   - (G) 4
   - (H) 5
   - (J) 6

 GO ON

Name _____   Date _____

MATH: APPLICATIONS

● **Lesson 12: Problem Solving (cont.)**

Hair Color	Boys							Girls						
Blonde														
Light Brown														
Dark Brown														
Red														
Black														
	1	2	3	4	5	6	7	1	2	3	4	5	6	7

Mrs. Garcia's class counted how many students had each different color of hair. They made a graph of their findings. Use the graph to answer the questions.

5. How many more girls have dark brown hair than boys?
- (A) 2
- (B) 4
- (C) 6
- (D) 8

6. How many boys and girls have light brown hair?
- (F) 11
- (G) 9
- (H) 12
- (J) 8

7. How many students are in the class?
- (A) 29
- (B) 15
- (C) 25
- (D) 31

8. How many more girls are in the class than boys?
- (F) 1
- (G) 2
- (H) 3
- (J) 4

9. What color of hair does only 1 student have?
- (A) blonde
- (B) red
- (C) light brown
- (D) black

10. How many more boys have dark brown hair than blonde hair?
- (F) 2
- (G) 0
- (H) 3
- (J) 5

GO ON

Name _____ Date _____

Our class is learning how to make winter bird feeders. For each feeder we need a small milk carton; a little peanut butter to help the seeds stick to the milk carton; one cup of birdseed; and some fishing line for hanging the feeder.

11. **How many cups of birdseed will we need to make 24 bird feeders?**

    Ⓐ 24
    Ⓑ 48
    Ⓒ 12
    Ⓓ 10

12. **If a bag of birdseed contains 30 cups and our class makes 24 feeders, how many cups of seed will be left?**

    Ⓕ 3
    Ⓖ 5
    Ⓗ 6
    Ⓙ 8

13. **If the birdseed costs $9.00 per bag, how much does 1 cup of seed cost?**

    Ⓐ $0.10
    Ⓑ $0.20
    Ⓒ $0.30
    Ⓓ $0.40

    1b = 30 c
    1b = $9.00

    $$3\overline{)9}\quad 3\overline{)90}$$

14. **The peanut butter costs $3.00 for a large jar. The fishing line is $4.00, and each milk carton is free. What is the total amount spent on supplies? (Don't forget to add in the cost of the birdseed.)**

    Ⓕ $11.00
    Ⓖ $23.00
    Ⓗ $16.00
    Ⓙ $19.00

15. **Each bird feeder will need 3 feet of fishing line. How much fishing line do they need all together?**

    Ⓐ 12
    Ⓑ 24
    Ⓒ 48
    Ⓓ 72

16. **Each bird feeder will need approximately 1 ounce of peanut butter. The peanut butter comes in four different size jars : 5 oz., 10 oz., 24 oz., and 48 oz. Which size jar should the class buy?**

    Ⓕ 5 oz.
    Ⓖ 10 oz.
    Ⓗ 24 oz.
    Ⓙ 48 oz.

GO ON

MATH: APPLICATIONS

● **Lesson 12: Problem Solving (cont.)**

Brett's school had a Science Fair every spring. He liked helping his teacher set up the exhibits.

17. Brett worked from 9:00 to 9:30. Later he helped for another hour. How many hours did Brett work?

- (A) 1/2 hour
- (B) 1 hour
- (C) 1 1/2 hours
- (D) 2 hours

18. Brett set three exhibits on one table. He decided to move one to another table that had four items. How many items were there on both tables all together?

- (F) 5
- (G) 7
- (H) 9
- (J) 11

19. Brett counted 10 exhibits about rocks. Then he saw 8 more about rocks. Three of the rock exhibits were blue-ribbon winners. How many were not?

- (A) 5
- (B) 10
- (C) 15
- (D) 20

20. Brett's teacher told him to put the 6 exhibits about water, the 7 about electricity, and the 1 about air pressure on two tables. He put the same number on each table. How many exhibits were on each table?

- (F) 5
- (G) 6
- (H) 7
- (J) 8

21. At the end of the science fair week, Brett's teacher asked him to help the 6 children that did water exhibits pack up their displays. She asked Marisa to help the 7 who did electricity exhibits, and Denny to help the 10 children who did exhibits about rocks. How many more exhibits did Marisa and Brett help with in total than Denny?

- (A) 0
- (B) 1
- (C) 2
- (D) 3

22. After the science fair projects were taken care of, Brett's teacher gave him and 4 other students 6 pieces of candy each for helping. How many pieces did they get altogether?

- (F) 20
- (G) 30
- (H) 45
- (J) 50

STOP

Name _____ Date_____

MATH: APPLICATIONS
SAMPLE TEST

● **Directions:** Listen to the questions. Choose the best answer to each question.

Example

A. Which picture looks the most like a circle?

 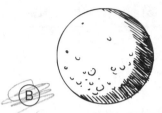  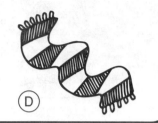

Ⓐ   Ⓑ   Ⓒ   Ⓓ

Use key words, pictures, and numbers to help you find the answer.

1. How many of these shapes have four or more sides?

Ⓐ 2
Ⓑ 3
Ⓒ 4
Ⓓ 5

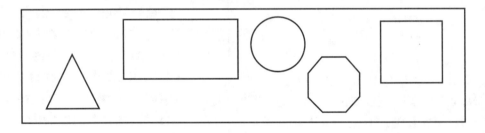

2. Which clock reads 11:15?

  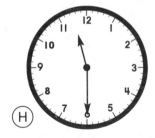 

Ⓕ   Ⓖ   Ⓗ   Ⓙ

3. How many more cones are there than cubes?

Ⓐ 2
Ⓑ 3
Ⓒ 4
Ⓓ 5

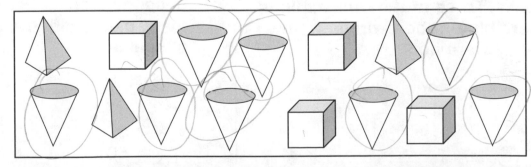

GO ON

Name _____   Date_____

4. What is the perimeter of this figure?

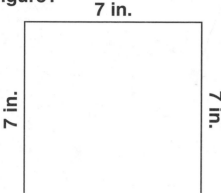

7 in.

7 in.

7 in.

7 in.

- (F) 28
- (G) 14
- (H) 32
- (J) 21

5. The first clock shows the time the students started the science experiment. The second clock shows when it ended. How long did the science experiment last?

- (A) 20 minutes
- (B) 30 minutes
- (C) 1 hour
- (D) 2 hours

6. Pretend you have the money below. Then you find 6 pennies. How much would you have?

- (F) 50¢
- (G) $1.06
- (H) $2.00
- (J) $2.10

7. Look at the calendar. How many Fridays are in July?

July

Sunday	Monday	Tuesday	Wednesday	Thursday	Friday	Saturday
		1	2	3	4	5
6	7	8	9	10	11	12
13	14	15	16	17	18	19
20	21	22	23	24	25	26
27	28	29	30	31		

- (A) 4
- (B) 5
- (C) 6
- (D) 0

GO ON

Name _____ Date _____

Animals We Saw

Name of Student	# of Pigs	# of Goats	# of Cows	# of Horses	# of Sheep
Sarah	2	1	6	2	2
David	6	1	5	4	4
Lisa	3	0	7	3	3
Josh	4	2	4	2	4
Madeline	3	1	9	3	2

Mrs. Harrow's second-grade class went on a field trip. They were told to count the number of animals they saw at the farm.

8. **How many fewer pigs did Madeline see than David?**

 (F) 2
 (G) 3
 (H) 4
 (J) 5

9. **How many cows, horses, and sheep did Josh see?**

 (A) 10
 (B) 8
 (C) 7
 (D) 6

10. **Who saw the most horses?**

 (F) Sarah
 (G) Lisa
 (H) Josh
 (J) David

11. **Who saw a total of 10 cows and horses?**

 (A) Sarah
 (B) Josh
 (C) Lisa
 (D) Madeline

12. **Who saw an equal number of goats?**

 (F) Sarah and Lisa
 (G) Lisa and Josh
 (H) Sarah, David, and Madeline
 (J) Sarah and Josh

13. **How many fewer goats did Sarah see than cows?**

 (A) 2
 (B) 4
 (C) 5
 (D) 3

GO ON

1-57768-722-1 *Spectrum Test Practice 2*

Mary and Ella are making pizza for their friends. They have just finished putting on the cheese. Now they need to bake it for 4 minutes.

14. What tool can you use to measure the cooking time?

(F) thermometer

(G) ruler

(H) stop watch

(J) measuring cup

15. If they put the pizza in the oven at 11:32, when will it be ready to come out?

(A) 10:30

(B) 11:35

(C) 11:36

(D) 11:40

16. The pizza has to feed 4 people. What fraction of the pizza will each person get?

(F) $\frac{1}{3}$

(G) $\frac{1}{2}$

(H) $\frac{2}{3}$

(J) $\frac{1}{4}$

17. If the pizza costs $4.00 to make, how much will each person owe if they split the cost evenly?

(A) 50¢

(B) $4.00

(C) $1.00

(D) $2.00

18. If Ella and Mary ordered a pizza to be delivered, it would cost $10.00 plus a $3.00 tip. How much money did they save by making it themselves?

(F) $4.00

(G) $9.00

(H) $12.00

(J) $13.00

19. Ella and Mary make sure they put on toppings that everyone would like. The toppings they had to choose from were pepperoni, sausage, tomatoes, onions, extra cheese, mushrooms, olives, and green peppers. Michael doesn't like tomatoes. Brian dislikes onions and green peppers. Mary and Ella only eat vegetables on their pizza. What toppings did Mary and Ella put on the pizza?

(A) pepperoni, extra cheese, and mushrooms

(B) olives and sausage

(C) only onions

(D) extra cheese, mushrooms, and olives

STOP

ANSWER SHEET

STUDENT'S NAME

LAST	FIRST	MI

LAST: L i n g

FIRST: C h r i s y

SCHOOL: Mount Prospect

TEACHER: Murphy

FEMALE ⬤   MALE ○

BIRTH DATE

MONTH	DAY	YEAR
May	4th	2004

MONTH: JAN, FEB, MAR, APR, MAY ⬤, JUN, JUL, AUG, SEP, OCT, NOV, DEC

GRADE
① ② ③

Part 1: CONCEPTS

A	Ⓐ Ⓑ Ⓒ Ⓓ
1	Ⓐ Ⓑ Ⓒ Ⓓ
2	Ⓕ Ⓖ Ⓗ Ⓙ
3	Ⓐ Ⓑ Ⓒ Ⓓ
4	Ⓕ Ⓖ Ⓗ Ⓙ
5	Ⓐ Ⓑ Ⓒ Ⓓ
6	Ⓕ Ⓖ Ⓗ Ⓙ
7	Ⓐ Ⓑ Ⓒ Ⓓ
8	Ⓕ Ⓖ Ⓗ Ⓙ
9	Ⓐ Ⓑ Ⓒ Ⓓ
10	Ⓕ Ⓖ Ⓗ Ⓙ
11	Ⓐ Ⓑ Ⓒ Ⓓ
12	Ⓕ Ⓖ Ⓗ Ⓙ
13	Ⓐ Ⓑ Ⓒ Ⓓ
14	Ⓕ Ⓖ Ⓗ Ⓙ
15	Ⓐ Ⓑ Ⓒ Ⓓ
16	Ⓕ Ⓖ Ⓗ Ⓙ

Part 2: COMPUTATION

A	Ⓐ Ⓑ Ⓒ Ⓓ
B	Ⓕ Ⓖ Ⓗ Ⓙ
1	Ⓐ Ⓑ Ⓒ Ⓓ
2	Ⓕ Ⓖ Ⓗ Ⓙ
3	Ⓐ Ⓑ Ⓒ Ⓓ
4	Ⓕ Ⓖ Ⓗ Ⓙ
5	Ⓐ Ⓑ Ⓒ Ⓓ
6	Ⓕ Ⓖ Ⓗ Ⓙ
7	Ⓐ Ⓑ Ⓒ Ⓓ
8	Ⓕ Ⓖ Ⓗ Ⓙ
9	Ⓐ Ⓑ Ⓒ Ⓓ
10	Ⓕ Ⓖ Ⓗ Ⓙ
11	Ⓐ Ⓑ Ⓒ Ⓓ
12	Ⓕ Ⓖ Ⓗ Ⓙ

Part 2: APPLICATIONS

A	Ⓐ Ⓑ Ⓒ Ⓓ
1	Ⓐ Ⓑ Ⓒ Ⓓ
2	Ⓕ Ⓖ Ⓗ Ⓙ
3	Ⓐ Ⓑ Ⓒ Ⓓ
4	Ⓕ Ⓖ Ⓗ Ⓙ
5	Ⓐ Ⓑ Ⓒ Ⓓ
6	Ⓕ Ⓖ Ⓗ Ⓙ
7	Ⓐ Ⓑ Ⓒ Ⓓ
8	Ⓕ Ⓖ Ⓗ Ⓙ
9	Ⓐ Ⓑ Ⓒ Ⓓ
10	Ⓕ Ⓖ Ⓗ Ⓙ
11	Ⓐ Ⓑ Ⓒ Ⓓ
12	Ⓕ Ⓖ Ⓗ Ⓙ
13	Ⓐ Ⓑ Ⓒ Ⓓ
14	Ⓕ Ⓖ Ⓗ
15	Ⓐ Ⓑ Ⓒ
16	Ⓕ Ⓖ Ⓗ
17	Ⓐ Ⓑ Ⓒ
18	Ⓕ Ⓖ Ⓗ
19	Ⓐ Ⓑ Ⓒ

1-57768-722-1 *Spectrum Test Practice 2*

MATH PRACTICE TEST

● **Part 1: Concepts**

Directions: Listen to each question. Choose the best answer.

Example

A. **Which shows the expanded numeral for one hundred eighty-three?**

(A) 200 + 83

(B) 100 + 180 + 30

(C) 100 + 80 + 3

(D) 108 +70 + 30

1. **Look at the number line. Which numeral should replace the circle?**

(A) 2

(B) 13

(C) 4

(D) 5

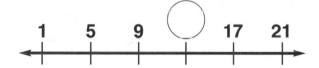

2. **Look at the hundreds, tens, and ones chart. What number is shown on the chart?**

(F) 745

(G) 935

(H) 835

(J) 837

100s	10s	1s
●● ●● ●● ●●	●● ●	●● ●● ●

3. **Which shape is ninth from the triangle?**

(A) circle

(B) square

(C) rectangle

(D) triangle

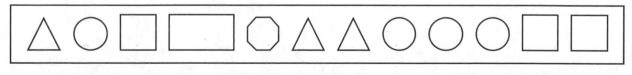

GO ON

● **Part 1: Concepts (cont.)**

4. Which fraction shows how much of the bar is not shaded?

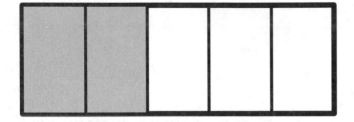

- (F) $\frac{1}{2}$
- (G) $\frac{1}{4}$
- (H) $\frac{3}{5}$
- (J) $\frac{2}{5}$

5. Which number is three hundred twenty-nine?

- (A) 3,029
- (B) 300,029
- (C) 3,290
- (D) 329

6. Look at the pattern. Which shape comes next?

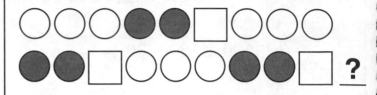

- (F)
- (G)
- (H) △
- (J) □

7. Which number should go in the boxes to make both number sentences true?

$$8 + \square = 22$$

$$22 - \square = 8$$

- (A) 12
- (B) 16
- (C) 14
- (D) 18

1-57768-722-1 *Spectrum Test Practice 2*

● **Part 1: Concepts (cont.)**

8. Look at the base ten blocks. How many are there total?

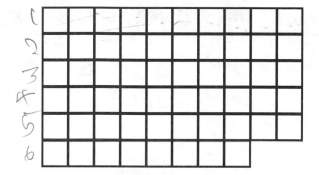

- (F) 55
- (G) 58
- (H) 62
- (J) 68

9. Which symbol goes in the number sentence to make it true?

$$15 \ \square \ 19 = 34$$

- (A) +
- (B) −
- (C) x
- (D) ÷

10. Which number is between 23 and 34?

- (F) 19
- (G) 40
- (H) 30
- (J) 20

11. Which number is missing from this number sequence?

$$19, \ 24, \ \_\_\_\_, \ 34, \ 39$$

- (A) 26
- (B) 29
- (C) 31
- (D) 32

GO ON

MATH PRACTICE TEST

● **Part 1: Concepts (cont.)**

12. How many of these problems have an answer of 12?

5	7	32	26	11
+ 7	+ 6	− 12	− 14	+ 6

- Ⓕ 1
- Ⓖ 2
- Ⓗ 3
- Ⓙ 4

13. Which number word fits in the blank to complete the pattern?

twenty-eight, twenty-nine, _____, thirty-one

- Ⓐ thirty-one
- Ⓑ thirty-nine
- Ⓒ thirty
- Ⓓ twenty-nine

14. Which number matches the number word in the box?

seven thousand, three hundred four

- Ⓕ 70,340
- Ⓖ 7,340
- Ⓗ 7,304
- Ⓙ 734

15. Which multiplication fact is shown by the dots in the box?

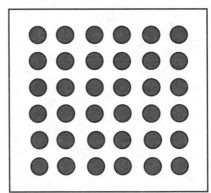

- Ⓐ 6 x 6 = 36
- Ⓑ 5 x 6 = 30
- Ⓒ 5 x 4 = 20
- Ⓓ 6 x 7 = 42

16. Which one shows the expanded numeral for five hundred thirty-three?

- Ⓕ 530 + 30 + 3
- Ⓖ 500 + 30 + 33
- Ⓗ 503 + 33
- Ⓙ 500 + 30 + 3

STOP

Name _____ Date _____

● **Part 2: Computation**

Directions: Solve each addition problem. Choose the best answer.

> **Examples**

This one has been done for you.	Practice on this one.
A. 3 + 9	B. $16 - 5 = \square$

This one has been done for you.

A.   3
    + 9

   (A) 15
   (B) 12
   (C) 10
   (D) 27

Practice on this one.

B. $16 - 5 = \square$

   (F) 11
   (G) 9
   (H) 10
   (J) 8

1.   63
    + 56

   (A) 109
   (B) 119
   (C) 19
   (D) 39

4.   489
    − 26
    463

   (F) 463
   (G) 466
   (H) 515
   (J) 415

2. $52 + 16 = \square$

   (F) 78
   (G) 68
   (H) 82
   (J) 64

5.   600
    − 30

   (A) 70
   (B) 670
   (C) 570
   (D) 630

3. $623 + 19 = \square$

   (A) 604
   (B) 652
   (C) 642
   (D) 504

6. $66 - 18 = \square$

   (F) 83
   (G) 84
   (H) 38
   (J) 48

GO ON →

MATH PRACTICE TEST

● **Part 2: Computation (cont.)**

7. $0.95
   + $0.12
   $1.07

(A) $1.07
(B) 17¢
(C) 77¢
(D) $10.77

10.   6)48
    8
   48
   0

(F) 54
(G) 42
(H) 8
(J) 7

8.   8 + 6 + 4 + 6 = □

(F) 19
(G) 22
(H) 24
(J) 34

11.   4
    x 8

(A) 32
(B) 12
(C) 4
(D) 28

9.   15 ÷ 3 = □

(A) 3
(B) 18
(C) 5
(D) 12

12.   7 x 7 = □

(F) 36
(G) 49
(H) 14
(J) 17

STOP

MATH PRACTICE TEST

● **Part 3: Applications**

Directions: Listen to the questions. Choose the best answer to each question.

Example

A. Pretend you have a dollar and buy a can of soda. This shows the change you received. How much did the soda cost?

Ⓐ 56¢
Ⓑ 43¢
Ⓒ 44¢
Ⓓ 29¢

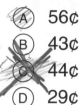    

1. Which shape can be folded in half so the parts match exactly?

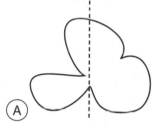 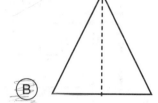 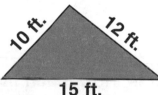 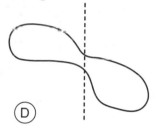

Ⓐ   Ⓑ   Ⓒ   Ⓓ

2. What is the perimeter of the figure?

Ⓕ 30 ft.
Ⓖ 27 ft.
Ⓗ 37 ft.
Ⓙ 25 ft.

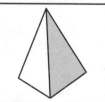

3. Look at the figure in the box. What word matches the figure?

Ⓐ cylinder
Ⓑ cube
Ⓒ sphere
Ⓓ pyramid

4. What shape would you have if you cut the kite in half?

Ⓕ   Ⓖ   Ⓗ   Ⓙ

GO ON

● **Part 3: Applications (cont.)**

5. **Which clock shows the time that is almost 8:15?**

 (A)   (B)    (C)    (D)

6. **Look at the calendar. What is the date of the third Wednesday in February?**

   (F) February 19
   (G) February 12
   (H) February 17
   (J) February 6

February						
Sunday	Monday	Tuesday	Wednesday	Thursday	Friday	Saturday
						1
2	3	4	5	6	7	8
9	10	11	12	13	14	15
16	17	18	19	20	21	22
23	23	25	26	27	28	

7. **Look at these coins. How much money do they show?**

   (A) $1.05
   (B) $1.00
   (C) 95¢
   (D) 99¢

8. **Which object costs the least?**

 $378⁰⁰    $39⁰⁰    $25⁰⁰    $212⁰⁰

   (F)   (G)   (H)   (J)   GO ON

1-57768-722-1 *Spectrum Test Practice 2*

MATH PRACTICE TEST

● **Part 3: Applications (cont.)**

9. How many fish long is the chain?

    (A) 6 fish
    (B) 2 fish
    (C) 5 fish
    (D) 8 fish

10. Which one of these objects weighs about 2 pounds?

    (F)   (G)   (H)

11. Shawna is 47 inches tall. Her little sister is 32 inches tall. How much taller is Shawna than her little sister?

    (A) 16 inches
    (B) 20 inches
    (C) 15 inches
    (D) 10 inches

12. The rug in the playroom needs to be replaced. Two of its sides are 72 inches each, and the other 2 sides are 100 inches each. What is the perimeter of the rug?

    (F) 344 inches
    (G) 400 inches
    (H) 272 inches
    (J) 144 inches

    72
    x 2
    ───
    144

    144
    +200
    ────
    344

13. In the morning, the temperature was 32 degrees. In the afternoon, it rose to 60 degrees. How many degrees warmer was it in the afternoon?

    (A) 28 degrees
    (B) 19 degrees
    (C) 82 degrees
    (D) 30 degrees

    GO ON

147 1-57768-722-1 *Spectrum Test Practice 2*

MATH PRACTICE TEST

● **Part 3: Applications (cont.)**

Birthdays	🧒 = one girl 🧒 = one boy			
January	🧒 🧒 🧒	July	🧒 🧒	
February	🧒	August	🧒 🧒	
March	🧒 🧒 🧒	September	🧒 🧒 🧒 🧒	
April	🧒 🧒 🧒 🧒	October	🧒 🧒 🧒 🧒	
May	🧒 🧒 🧒	November	🧒 🧒	
June		December		

Mr. Hamm's class made a graph of how many students in the class had birthdays in each month. Use the graph to answer the questions.

14. How many students have birthdays in March and April?
- (F) 6
- (G) 7
- (H) 8

15. What fraction of birthdays in September are boys'?
- (A) $\frac{1}{2}$
- (B) $\frac{1}{4}$
- (C) $\frac{3}{4}$

16. How many more students have birthdays in October than in February?
- (F) 2
- (G) 3
- (H) 4

17. How many students have birthdays during the summer months?
- (A) 4
- (B) 6
- (C) 8

18. In which months do only girls have birthdays?
- (F) November and December
- (G) August and November
- (H) February and July

19. Which month has the least number of birthdays?
- (A) November
- (B) February
- (D) December

STOP

Name _____ Date_____

SCIENCE

● **Lesson 1: Science**

Directions: Read or listen to the passage. Choose the best answers to the questions.

Example

My Skeleton

You cannot see many things inside of you. However, you can feel some things. Feel your head. Feel your fingers. Feel your knees. They are hard. They have bones. Bones make up your skeleton. Your skeleton gives you shape. If you had no bones, you would be like a rag doll!

A. **What does your skeleton give you?**

- (A) money
- (B) food
- (C) breath
- (D) shape

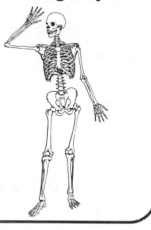

 **Clue** Think about the question and look at all the choices before you choose an answer.

● **Practice**

Our Atmosphere

All around our world is a thick layer of air. We call it our atmosphere. It is always changing. It can be hot or cold. It can be wet or dry. This change in atmosphere is called weather.

The sun causes weather. The sun causes wind, rain, clouds, and snow. Weather happens only in our layer of air. There is no weather in outer space.

1. **What is our layer of air closest to the earth called?**
   - (A) weather
   - (B) atmosphere
   - (C) climate
   - (D) mountains

2. **What is it called when the atmosphere changes?**
   - (F) weather
   - (G) atmosphere
   - (H) dry
   - (J) hot

3. **What causes weather?**
   - (A) moon
   - (B) mountains
   - (C) sun
   - (D) snow

4. **Where is there no weather?**
   - (F) on the top of mountains
   - (G) in valleys
   - (H) in outer space
   - (J) in fields

SCIENCE

● **Lesson 2: Science**

The Water Cycle

The dark clouds begin to rain. The rain falls on the grass and the streets, making puddles. It falls on the hills, running down in little streams. They flow into lakes and then to the ocean.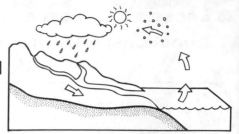

The rain is over. Out peeks the sun. The water in the puddles, streams, lakes, and ocean gets warm. Some changes to vapor, like steam rising out of a boiling teakettle. It disappears into the air.

Warm air rises, so up it goes. The air is cooler here. There are specks of dust. When the vapor hits a cool speck, it sticks to it and condenses. These bits of dust and water drops come together to make clouds. When they are heavy with water, down comes the rain again.

1. **Why is the process described as a cycle?**
    - (A) because the process stops fast
    - (B) because the process happens over and over again
    - (C) because the process doesn't start fast
    - (D) because the process happens only once every year

2. **What falls from dark clouds?**
    - (F) sunshine
    - (G) frogs
    - (H) rain
    - (J) hot weather

3. **What warms the water?**
    - (A) sun
    - (B) moon
    - (C) stars
    - (D) an electric heater

4. **What happens when water warms?**
    - (F) It changes to vapor, rises, and disappears into the air.
    - (G) It falls on hills and makes streams.
    - (H) It sticks to dust.
    - (J) It flows into lakes and ocean.

5. **What would happen if there were no specks of dust?**
    - (A) The sun would shine brighter.
    - (B) The moon would disappear.
    - (C) There would be no clouds.
    - (D) Rain puddles wouldn't form.

6. **Vapor is described as "steam rising out of a boiling teakettle." What is another example to describe vapor?**
    - (F) ice freezing in a cup
    - (G) warm air hitting cold glass causing water to form
    - (H) snow melting outside
    - (J) water heating causing it to turn into a gas

Name _____ Date _____

SOCIAL STUDIES

● **Lesson 1: Social Studies**

Directions: Read or listen to the passage. Choose the best answers to the questions.

Example

Washington, District of Columbia

Washington is the capital city of the United States. The land around the city is called the District of Columbia (D.C.). It belongs to the United States government.

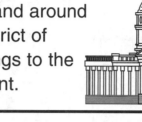

A. What does D.C. stand for?

- (A) Don't you Cut
- (B) Douglas Columbus
- (C) Down too Close
- (D) District of Columbia

 Clue Think about the question and look at all the choices before you choose an answer.

● **Practice**

Our Constitution

The Constitution is a document or official paper. It tells about the government of the United States. It also tells about rights and freedoms of the American people.

In 1787, America's leaders had a meeting. They met at Independence Hall in Philadelphia, Pennsylvania. While they were there, they wrote the Constitution. Then they signed it. Today, the Constitution is kept in the National Archives in Washington, D.C.

1. What is the Constitution?
- (A) a law that tells what to do
- (B) a story written long ago
- (C) a government
- (D) an official paper that tells about freedom of Americans

2. What two things does the Constitution tell?
- (F) place and time
- (G) the money that was spent
- (H) about the government and freedom
- (J) about other countries and war

3. When was the Constitution written?
- (A) 1983
- (B) 1787
- (C) 1789
- (D) 1857

4. Why is the Constitution kept in the National Archives?
- (F) because there are many copies
- (G) because it is important
- (H) because it once was lost
- (J) because of Washington

ANSWER SHEET

STUDENT'S NAME

LAST: Ling

FIRST: Chrisy

MI

SCHOOL: Mount Prospect

TEACHER: Mrs. Murphy

FEMALE ●   MALE ○

BIRTH DATE

MONTH	DAY	YEAR
May	4	2004

MONTH: MAY ●

DAY: 4

YEAR: 2004

GRADE

① ② ③ (3 filled)

SCIENCE AND SOCIAL STUDIES

A Ⓐ Ⓑ Ⓒ Ⓓ   5 Ⓐ Ⓑ Ⓒ Ⓓ
1 Ⓐ Ⓑ Ⓒ Ⓓ   6 Ⓕ Ⓖ Ⓗ Ⓙ
2 Ⓕ Ⓖ Ⓗ Ⓙ

Name _____ Date _____

Directions: Read or listen to the passage. Then answer the questions.

Example

Fire Safety

If someone's clothes catch on fire, they shouldn't run or walk anywhere. They should stop, drop to the ground, and roll around to put the fire out.

A. **What should someone do if their clothes catch on fire?**

- (A) stop, drop, and run fast
- (B) walk to get help
- (C) sit and wait for help
- (D) stop, drop, and roll

What Is a Bird?

A bird is an animal with feathers. Feathers protect a bird's skin and help it keep warm. Feathers also help to waterproof a bird's body.

A bird has two legs and a hard beak. It also has many bones that are hollow like a straw. These bones make the bird lighter and better able to fly. Some birds, such as the penguin, cannot fly.

Every bird hatches from an egg. The egg is kept warm by the father or mother bird. When the young bird hatches, its parents usually feed it.

1. **What would happen if the father and mother bird did not keep the egg warm?**
   - (A) It would hatch sooner.
   - (B) The baby bird would be sad.
   - (C) The father and mother would be upset.
   - (D) The egg wouldn't hatch.

2. **How do feathers help birds?**
   - (F) They help them think.
   - (G) They help protect them and keep them warm.
   - (H) They help other birds see.
   - (J) They help them feel where they are going.

3. **Write how hollow bones help birds.**

   They make the bird lighter and able to fly.

4. **Write about your favorite bird. Tell why it is your favorite.**

   Bluejay because they are really cute.

   GO ON ▷

SCIENCE AND SOCIAL STUDIES PRACTICE TEST

Directions: Read or listen to the passage. Then answer the questions.

Around the Globe

You know that the earth is not flat. It is a very big ball, or sphere. Imagine being able to cut the earth in half, in the same way you cut an orange. The halves are called **hemispheres**. Hemisphere means "half-ball." Depending on how you divide the earth, up and down or across the middle, North America will either be in the Western Hemisphere or in Northern Hemisphere.

The world can also be divided into seven large land masses. These big areas are called **continents**. Their names are Asia, Africa, Europe, North America, South America, Australia, and Antarctica. Asia is the largest continent. More than half of the world's people live there. No one lives on Antarctica because it's too cold!

5. **What is a continent?**
   - (A) where you divide a country
   - (B) countries that have too many people
   - (C) a space on the sun
   - (D) giant areas of land

6. **Which is not a continent?**
   - (F) Northern Hemisphere
   - (G) North America
   - (H) Europe
   - (J) Australia

7. **Write about what you would do and where you would go if you could visit a different continent.**

   I would go to Asia so I can explore the huge country, China.

8. **Write about the different ways to divide our world.**

   It can be divided in half or in seven continents.

STOP

ANSWER KEY

READING: WORD ANALYSIS
Lesson 1: Word Sounds
• Page 11
- A. B
- 1. A
- 2. H
- 3. C
- 4. F
- 5. B
- 6. F

READING: WORD ANALYSIS
Lesson 2: Rhyming Words
• Page 12
- A. A
- 1. A
- 2. G
- 3. B
- 4. H

READING: WORD ANALYSIS
Lesson 3: Word Sounds
• Page 13
- A. C
- B. G
- 1. A
- 2. J
- 3. B
- 4. H
- 5. B
- 6. F

READING: WORD ANALYSIS
Lesson 4: Rhyming Words
• Page 14
- A. C
- B. B
- 1. C
- 2. H
- 3. A
- 4. G

READING: WORD ANALYSIS
Lesson 5: Contractions and Compound Words
• Page 15
- A. A
- B. F
- 1. D
- 2. G
- 3. D
- 4. J
- 5. B
- 6. H

READING: WORD ANALYSIS
Lesson 6: Root Words and Suffixes
• Page 16
- A. D
- B. H
- 1. C
- 2. F

- 3. B
- 4. H
- 5. D
- 6. H

READING: WORD ANALYSIS
Sample Test
• Pages 17–20
- A. B
- 1. B
- 2. F
- 3. B
- 4. H
- 5. B
- 6. G
- B. H
- 7. C
- 8. G
- 9. C
- 10. F
- C. B
- D. H
- 11. A
- 12. H
- 13. D
- 14. G
- 15. C
- 16. J
- E. D
- F. G
- 17. B
- 18. F
- 19. D
- 20. F
- 21. B
- 22. J

READING: VOCABULARY
Lesson 7: Picture Vocabulary
• Page 21
- A. B
- B. F
- 1. C
- 2. F
- 3. D
- 4. H

READING: VOCABULARY
Lesson 8: Word Meaning
• Page 22
- A. D
- 1. A
- 2. H
- 3. D
- 4. G
- 5. B
- 6. F

READING: VOCABULARY
Lesson 9: Synonyms
• Page 23
- A. D
- 1. C
- 2. J
- 3. B
- 4. F
- 5. A
- 6. J

READING: VOCABULARY
Lesson 10: Antonyms
• Page 24
- A. C
- 1. D
- 2. H
- 3. B
- 4. F
- 5. C
- 6. H

READING: VOCABULARY
Lesson 11: Words in Context
• Page 25
- A. B
- B. F
- 1. B
- 2. H
- 3. A
- 4. H

READING: VOCABULARY
Lesson 12: Multiple Meaning Words
• Page 26
- A. D
- 1. A
- 2. H
- 3. B
- 4. J
- 5. C

READING: VOCABULARY
Sample Test
• Pages 27–30
- A. D
- 1. A
- 2. H
- 3. D
- 4. F
- B. H
- 5. B
- 6. G
- 7. A
- 8. H
- 9. D
- 10. F
- C. B
- D. F
- 11. B
- 12. G

13. D
14. F
15. C
16. G
E. C
F. G
17. A
18. H
19. A
20. F

READING: COMPREHENSION
Lesson 13: Picture Comprehension
• Page 31
A. B
1. A
2. H
3. D
4. F

READING: COMPREHENSION
Lesson 14: Critical Reading
• Page 32
A. D
1. B
2. J

READING: COMPREHENSION
Lesson 15: Fiction
• Pages 33–34
A. A
1. D
2. H
3. B
4. J
5. C
6. H
7. D
8. J

Lesson 16: Nonfiction
• Pages 35–36
1. C
2. J
3. B
4. H
5. A
6. H
7. C
8. J

READING: COMPREHENSION
Sample Test
• Pages 37–40
A. A
1. B
2. F
3. D
4. J
5. B
6. J
7. A

8. H
9. C
10. J
11. C
12. G
13. D
14. F
15. B
16. F

READING PRACTICE TEST
Part 1: Word Analysis
• Pages 42–45
A. B
1. B
2. H
3. C
4. J
5. C
6. J
B. J
C. B
7. A
8. J
9. C
10. G
11. B
12. F
D. H
E. C
13. A
14. H
15. B
16. G
F. F
G. A
17. C
18. H
19. D
20. G
21. A
22. F

READING PRACTICE TEST
Part 2: Vocabulary
• Pages 46–51
A. B
1. A
2. J
3. C
4. G
B. J
5. A
6. J
7. D
8. F
9. B
10. F
C. A

11. A
12. G
13. C
14. H
15. A
16. F
D. G
17. D
18. G
19. C
20. F
21. D
22. G
E. A
F. H
23. C
24. G
25. A
26. G
27. C
28. G
G. B
29. A
30. H
31. C
32. J
33. B
34. H

READING PRACTICE TEST
Part 3: Story Comprehension
• Pages 52–56
A. C
1. D
2. F
3. C
4. J
5. D
6. F
7. C
8. H
9. B
10. F
11. D
12. G
13. C
14. H
15. A
16. G
17. D
18. G
19. D
20. F

LANGUAGE: LISTENING
Lesson 1: Listening Skills
• Page 57
A. B
1. C

2. F
3. B

LANGUAGE: LISTENING
Lesson 2: Listening Skills
• Page 58
A. C
1. D
2. H
3. D
4. H
5. B
6. F

LANGUAGE: LISTENING
Sample Test
• Page 59
A. B
B. F
1. B
2. G
3. C
4. G
5. D
6. G

LANGUAGE: MECHANICS
Lesson 3: Capitalization
• Page 60
A. D
1. D
2. H
3. A
4. J
5. C
6. F

LANGUAGE: MECHANICS
Lesson 4: Punctuation
• Page 61
A. A
B. G
1. C
2. G
3. C
4. F
5. C
6. G

LANGUAGE: MECHANICS
Lesson 5: Capitalization
and Punctuation
• Pages 62–63
A. C
B. H
1. B
2. G
3. C
4. F
5. C
6. G
C. B

D. F
7. B
8. F
9. C
10. F

LANGUAGE: MECHANICS
Sample Test
• Pages 64–67
A. A
1. C
2. G
3. A
4. J
5. B
6. G
B. F
C. B
7. A
8. F
9. A
10. F
11. C
12. F
D. H
E. B
13. C
14. F
15. C
16. G
17. C
18. F
F. G
G. C
19. A
20. H
21. A
22. G

LANGUAGE: EXPRESSION
Lesson 6: Usage
• Page 68
A. D
B. G
1. C
2. F
3. D
4. G
5. D
6. H

LANGUAGE: EXPRESSION
Lesson 7: Usage
• Page 69
A. C
B. G
1. C
2. G
3. B
4. F

5. C
6. F

LANGUAGE: EXPRESSION
Lesson 8: Sentences
• Pages 70–71
A. B
1. A
2. H
3. D
4. G
5. C
6. J
B. F
7. C
8. J
9. A
10. G
11. A
12. H

LANGUAGE: EXPRESSION
Lesson 9: Paragraphs
• Pages 72–73
A. C
1. B
2. J
3. D
4. F
5. D
B. F
6. G
7. A
8. H
9. B

LANGUAGE: EXPRESSION
Sample Test
• Pages 74–76
A. B
B. H
1. C
2. J
3. A
4. J
5. C
6. G
C. C
7. D
8. F
9. D
10. G
11. D
12. G
D. G
13. A
14. G
15. C
16. H

ANSWER KEY

LANGUAGE: SPELLING
Lesson 10: Spelling Skills
• Page 77

- A. B
- 1. C
- 2. J
- 3. B
- 4. J
- 5. A
- 6. G

LANGUAGE: SPELLING
Lesson 11: Spelling Skills
• Page 78

- A. A
- 1. C
- 2. G
- 3. D
- 4. F
- 5. B
- 6. H

LANGUAGE: SPELLING
Lesson 12: Spelling Skills
• Page 79

- A. B
- 1. A
- 2. G
- 3. A
- 4. F
- 5. C
- 6. G

LANGUAGE: SPELLING
Sample Test
• Pages 80–82

- A. C
- 1. D
- 2. G
- 3. A
- 4. H
- 5. A
- 6. H
- B. F
- 7. D
- 8. F
- 9. C
- 10. G
- 11. C
- 12. G
- C. B
- 13. A
- 14. H
- 15. B
- 16. H
- 17. B
- 18. F

LANGUAGE: STUDY SKILLS
Lesson 13: Study Skills
• Pages 83–85

- A. C

- B. G
- 1. A
- 2. H
- C. A
- 3. D
- 4. J
- 5. A
- 6. G
- 7. B
- 8. J
- D. J
- 9. A
- 10. G
- 11. C
- 12. H
- 13. A
- 14. G

LANGUAGE: STUDY SKILLS
Sample Test
• Pages 86–87

- A. A
- B. J
- 1. D
- 2. H
- 3. B
- 4. G
- 5. D
- 6. F
- C. B
- 7. C
- 8. F
- 9. B
- 10. F

LANGUAGE PRACTICE TEST
Part 1: Listening
• Page 89

- A. C
- B. J
- 1. B
- 2. F
- 3. B
- 4. H
- 5. D

LANGUAGE PRACTICE TEST
Part 2: Language Mechanics
• Pages 90–91

- A. A
- B. H
- 1. B
- 2. F
- 3. C
- 4. G
- 5. A
- 6. G
- C. B
- D. F
- 7. C
- 8. F

- 9. A
- 10. F

LANGUAGE PRACTICE TEST
Part 3: Language Expression
• Pages 92–98

- A. B
- B. G
- 1. C
- 2. F
- 3. D
- 4. J
- 5. C
- 6. F
- C. A
- 7. C
- 8. F
- 9. B
- 10. H
- 11. A
- 12. G
- D. J
- 13. B
- 14. H
- 15. A
- 16. H
- 17. B
- 18. H
- E. C
- 19. A
- 20. G
- 21. D
- 22. G
- 23. C
- 24. F
- F. J
- 25. A
- 26. G
- 27. C
- 28. H
- 29. C
- 30. J
- G. C
- 31. A
- 32. G
- 33. B
- 34. F
- 35. A
- 36. G
- 37. C
- 38. F
- 39. C

LANGUAGE PRACTICE TEST
Part 4: Spelling
• Pages 99–100

- A. A
- 1. C
- 2. J
- 3. B

1-57768-722-1 *Spectrum Test Practice 2*

4. F
5. A
6. J
B. F
C. A
7. C
8. G
9. A
10. H
11. A
12. H

LANGUAGE PRACTICE TEST
Part 5: Study Skills
· Pages 101–102

A. B
B. J
1. A
2. F
3. C
4. F
5. D
6. J
C. A
7. A
8. G
9. C
10. G

MATH: CONCEPTS
Lesson 1: Numeration
· Pages 103–104

A. D
1. A
2. F
3. D
4. H
5. B
6. G
7. A
8. H
9. C

MATH: CONCEPTS
Lesson 2: Number Concepts
· Pages 105–106

A. D
1. B
2. F
3. C
4. G
5. B
6. J
7. B
8. H
9. A

MATH: CONCEPTS
Lesson 3: Patterns and Place Value
· Pages 107–108

A. D

1. C
2. G
3. D
4. H
5. B
6. F
7. B
8. H

MATH: CONCEPTS
Lesson 4: Properties
· Pages 109–110

A. D
1. D
2. G
3. B
4. J
5. A
6. G
7. D

MATH: CONCEPTS
Sample Test
· Pages 111–114

A. C
1. D
2. J
3. B
4. G
5. B
6. H
7. A
8. J
9. A
10. G
11. D
12. H
13. B
14. G
15. B

MATH: COMPUTATION
Lesson 5: Addition
· Pages 115–116

A. D
B. H
1. C
2. F
3. C
4. J
5. A
6. G
7. C
8. F
9. C
10. J

MATH: COMPUTATION
Lesson 6: Subtraction
· Pages 117–118

A. A

B. H
1. B
2. F
3. C
4. G
5. C
6. G
7. B
8. F
9. C
10. J

MATH: COMPUTATION
Lesson 7: Multiplication and Division
· Page 119

A. B
B. F
1. C
2. F
3. C
4. F

MATH: COMPUTATION
Sample Test
· Pages 120–121

A. B
B. G
1. B
2. H
3. D
4. F
5. C
6. G
7. A
8. G
9. D
10. F

MATH: APPLICATIONS
Lesson 8: Geometry
· Pages 122–123

A. B
1. C
2. G
3. C
4. G
5. D
6. H

MATH: APPLICATIONS
Lesson 9: Geometry
· Pages 124–125

A. D
1. B
2. F
3. D
4. J
5. C
6. G
7. B

MATH: APPLICATIONS
Lesson 10: Measurement
• Pages 126–127
- A. C
- 1. D
- 2. F
- 3. C
- 4. F
- 5. D
- 6. F
- 7. B
- 8. H

MATH: APPLICATIONS
Lesson 11: Measurement
• Pages 128–129
- A. D
- 1. D
- 2. F
- 3. C
- 4. F
- 5. C
- 6. F
- 7. D

MATH: APPLICATIONS
Lesson 12: Problem Solving
• Pages 130–133
- A. A
- 1. B
- 2. H
- 3. D
- 4. H
- 5. A
- 6. H
- 7. A
- 8. F
- 9. D
- 10. H
- 11. A
- 12. H
- 13. A
- 14. H
- 15. D
- 16. H
- 17. C
- 18. G
- 19. C
- 20. H
- 21. D
- 22. G

MATH: APPLICATIONS
Sample Test
• Pages 134–137
- A. B
- 1. B
- 2. J
- 3. C
- 4. F

- 5. C
- 6. G
- 7. A
- 8. G
- 9. A
- 10. J
- 11. C
- 12. H
- 13. C
- 14. H
- 15. C
- 16. J
- 17. C
- 18. G
- 19. D

MATH PRACTICE TEST
Part 1: Concepts
• Pages 139–142
- A. C
- 1. B
- 2. H
- 3. A
- 4. H
- 5. D
- 6. F
- 7. C
- 8. G
- 9. A
- 10. H
- 11. B
- 12. G
- 13. C
- 14. H
- 15. A
- 16. J

MATH PRACTICE TEST
Part 2: Computation
• Pages 143–144
- A. B
- B. F
- 1. B
- 2. G
- 3. C
- 4. F
- 5. C
- 6. J
- 7. A
- 8. H
- 9. C
- 10. H
- 11. A
- 12. G

MATH PRACTICE TEST
Part 3: Applications
• Pages 145–148
- A. A
- 1. B

- 2. H
- 3. D
- 4. H
- 5. C
- 6. F
- 7. D
- 8. H
- 9. C
- 10. J
- 11. C
- 12. F
- 13. A
- 14. G
- 15. C
- 16. G
- 17. B
- 18. G
- 19. C

SCIENCE
Lesson 1: Science
• Page 149
- A. D
- 1. B
- 2. F
- 3. C
- 4. H

SCIENCE
Lesson 2: Science
• Page 150
- 1. B
- 2. H
- 3. A
- 4. F
- 5. C
- 6. J

SOCIAL STUDIES
Lesson 1: Social Studies
• Page 151
- A. D
- 1. D
- 2. H
- 3. B
- 4. G

SCIENCE AND SOCIAL STUDIES PRACTICE TEST
• Pages 153–154
- A. D
- 1. D
- 2. G
- 3. They made the bird lighter and able to fly.
- 4. Answers will vary.
- 5. D
- 6. F
- 7. Answers will vary.
- 8. It can be divided in half or into seven continents.